T0286797

Cambridge Elements ≡

Elements in Political Economy
edited by
David Stasavage
New York University

BACKSLIDING

Democratic Regress in the Contemporary World

Stephan Haggard
Robert Kaufman

CAMBRIDGE
UNIVERSITY PRESS

CAMBRIDGE
UNIVERSITY PRESS

University Printing House, Cambridge CB2 8BS, United Kingdom

One Liberty Plaza, 20th Floor, New York, NY 10006, USA

477 Williamstown Road, Port Melbourne, VIC 3207, Australia

314–321, 3rd Floor, Plot 3, Splendor Forum, Jasola District Centre,
New Delhi – 110025, India

79 Anson Road, #06–04/06, Singapore 079906

Cambridge University Press is part of the University of Cambridge.

It furthers the University's mission by disseminating knowledge in the pursuit of
education, learning, and research at the highest international levels of excellence.

www.cambridge.org
Information on this title: www.cambridge.org/9781108958400
DOI: 10.1017/9781108957809

© Stephan Haggard and Robert Kaufman 2021

First published 2021

A catalogue record for this publication is available from the British Library.

ISBN 978-1-108-95840-0 Paperback
ISSN 2398-4031 (online)
ISSN 2514-3816 (print)

Backsliding

Democratic Regress in the Contemporary World

Elements in Political Economy

DOI: 10.1017/9781108957809
First published online: January 2021

Stephan Haggard
Robert Kaufman

Author for correspondence: Stephan Haggard, shaggard@uscd.edu

Abstract: Assaults on democracy are increasingly coming from the actions of duly elected governments, rather than coups. Backsliding examines the processes through which elected rulers weaken checks on executive power, curtail political and civil liberties, and undermine the integrity of the electoral system. Drawing on detailed case studies, including the United States and countries in Latin America, Eastern Europe, and Africa, this Element focuses on three, inter-related causal mechanisms: the pernicious effects of polarization; realignments of party systems that enable elected autocrats to gain legislative power; and the incremental nature of derogations, which divides oppositions and keeps them off balance. A concluding chapter looks at the international context of backsliding and the role of new technologies in these processes. An online appendix provides detailed accounts of backsliding in 16 countries, which can be found at www.cambridge.org/backsliding.

Keywords: Democracy, backsliding, authoritarianism, elections, polarization.

ISBNs: 9781108958400 (PB), 9781108957809 (OC)
ISSNs: 2398-4031 (online), 2514-3816 (print)

Contents

1 Backsliding: Concept, Mechanisms, Measurement   1

2 Social and Political Origins of Backsliding: The Role of Polarization   14

3 Constitutions in the Balance: Parties, Legislatures and the Collapse of the Separation of Powers   39

4 The Backsliding Process   56

5 Conclusion   78

References   85

1 Backsliding: Concept, Mechanisms, Measurement

The "Third Wave" of democratization (Huntington 1993) began in the mid-1970s in Portugal, Greece and Spain. It picked up steam in the 1980s in Latin America and a number of East Asian countries, gaining even greater strength in the 1990s with the collapse of the Soviet Union and the winding down of the Cold War. The expansion of electoral regimes throughout the world generated optimism, even triumphalism (Fukuyama 1989).

By the early 2000s, however, significant doubts had set in about whether the new democracies would last; or indeed, whether they should be considered democracies at all (Zakaria 1997; Carothers 2002; Diamond 2002; Schedler 2002; Ottaway 2003; Zakaria 2007; Schedler 2009; Levitsky & Way 2010) Many of the countries that did manage transitions to democracy proved unable to sustain them. What was distinctive and troubling about many of these reversions, moreover, was not simply that they occurred but the mechanisms through which they did so. Rather than abrupt changes of regime via the classic coup d'état, regression from democratic rule took place through a process that has come to be known as "backsliding" (Bermeo 2016; Mechkova, Lührmann & Lindberg 2017; Waldner & Lust 2018; Kaufman and Haggard 2019). By backsliding we mean the incremental erosion of democratic institutions, rules and norms that results from the actions of duly elected governments, typically driven by an autocratic leader. While backsliding may stop short of outright authoritarian rule, a number of cases did in fact revert. Democracy was consuming itself.

The regimes vulnerable to backsliding included not only "weak" democracies that had at best met minimal electoral criteria but also some middle-income countries, such as Hungary and Poland, where democracy appeared to have been consolidated; there were disturbing signs in other Eastern European democracies as well (Lindberg 2018). The threat, moreover, was not limited to middle-income countries. The 2016 election of Donald Trump in the United States challenged the widespread assumption that rich, liberal democracies were invulnerable and unleashed an unsettling conversation on whether "it could happen here" (Ginsburg and Huq 2018; Levitsky & Ziblatt 2018; Mounk 2018; Sunstein 2018a; Hennessey and Wittes 2020; and Graber, Levinson & Tushnet 2018 for legal perspectives). Western Europe was not immune either. The rise of right-wing populist parties on the continent and the bruising fight over Brexit sparked fears about the state of democracy in Western Europe (Golder 2016; Eatwell & Goodwin 2018). Did polarizing cleavages put the advanced industrial states at risk?

In this Element, we survey the phenomenon of democratic backsliding. We start in this section with the conceptual terrain and questions of measurement: how to capture the backsliding process and to identify plausible cases. Our empirical contribution rests on an analysis of backsliding episodes in sixteen countries, with structured case studies contained in the accompanying online Appendix.[1]

Our theoretical approach does not privilege any single variable but sees backsliding as the outcome of a complex causal chain; the links in that chain structure the volume. We start in Section 2 with polarization: the process through which polities increasingly divide not only over policy or ideology but over identity as well. We focus less on its causes – which are multiple – than on its pernicious effects. In Section 3 we consider how political polarization translates into the election of autocrats, with a focus on changes in the party system and within parties. However, we argue that control of the legislature is a crucial step in what we call the collapse of the separation of powers: the weakening of horizontal checks on executive discretion. In Section 4, we argue that the incremental nature of the backsliding process itself has causal effects, strengthening the power of executives and disorienting and disorganizing oppositions. In the concluding Section 5 we look forward to new areas for research, considering the role of international factors, the information landscape and the effects of crises such as the onset of the COVID-19 on backsliding processes.

1.1 Conceptual Issues: Backsliding from What to What?

Since we conceive of backsliding as a process in which democratically elected leaders weaken democratic institutions, certain cognate forms of regime change are excluded from consideration. Coups and executive *autogolpes* (self-coups) remain an important, if diminishing, threat to democracy (Powell & Thyne 2011; Bermeo 2016, 7–8; Geddes, Wright & Frantz 2018). But our concern here is with threats that come out of the constitutional process itself. As a result, we do not focus on cases in which military elites figure prominently in the process or in which abrupt civilian seizures of power occur. Rather, we focus more attention on the elected officials and contenders – presidents, prime ministers, legislators and other political elites – who deploy majoritarian appeals to undermine the institutional checks and protections of liberal democracy.

Backsliding must also be seen as distinctive in that it can lead to a deterioration in democratic rule that falls short of outright reversion to autocracy. This possibility was anticipated in the early 1970s in debates over

---

[1] The online Appendix can be found at www.cambridge.org/backsliding.

the "quality" of democracy in the advanced industrial states (e.g., Crozier, Huntington and Watanuki 1975; Lindblom 1977), as well as in more recent concerns about the inability to forge policy compromises and the resulting erosion of trust in government (e.g., Diamond & Morlino 2004; Mann & Ornstein 2012 on the United States). Our analysis builds on such concerns but focuses on *purposeful institutional change.* Although we too use the term "erosion" in a particular way, it is important to avoid natural metaphors and the passive tense. Backsliding results from the political strategies and tactics of autocratic leaders and their allies in the executive, legislative and judicial branches of government.

Changes in what, exactly? The concept of democracy has received more analytic scrutiny than any other in the field of political science, but the discussion continues to rotate around three mutually constitutive pillars that will also structure our analysis: free and fair elections; the protection of basic political rights and liberties; and the existence of horizontal checks on executive discretion, including what is known as the "rule of law."

A first pillar – for some the irreducible core of democracy – lies in the electoral process (Schumpter 1962; Przeworski, Stokes & Manin 1999; Przeworski 2019). Democracy is grounded in the conduct of free and fair elections that permit turnover and thus assure relationships of "vertical" accountability. As the ability for oppositions to take office falls toward zero, democracy is effectively overthrown, and reversion to some form of authoritarian rule has therefore occurred. The decline in the integrity of the electoral system can occur in a myriad of ways: efforts to restrict the franchise and to suppress the vote through onerous registration or voting laws; disinformation campaigns that mislead voters about their voting rights; interference in the integrity of election monitoring; and outright fraud (see Norris 2014 for a catalogue).

An equally strong case can be made that the protection of basic political rights and civil liberties is democracy's irreducible core. Without protections for the fundamental rights of speech, assembly and association, civil society organizations, oppositions and even political parties could not form. Protection of the media is a crucial component of this pillar of democratic rule. Although we focus primarily on core political rights, we will show that backsliding is often associated with demonization of adversaries and assaults on the rights of ethnic, racial, religious or sexual minorities as well.

Finally, we underline the importance of horizontal checks in any definition of liberal democracy (Schedler 1999; Ginsburg and Huq 2018). The concept of constitutionalism has at its heart the paradox of self-limiting government (Elster 1988): that electoral majorities must have incentives to temper their power through continued submission to electoral scrutiny, checks and the rule of law. The most fundamental separation of powers – between the executive, legislature and judicial branches – has a pedigree that can be traced to Montesquieu and *The Federalist Papers*. Backsliding typically involves what we call a "collapse in the separation of powers" between branches of government as the executive gains control of other branches, most importantly through appointment of loyalists and sycophants (on authoritarian constitutionalism, see Ginsburg and Simpser 2014; Graber, Levinson & Tushnet 2015; Tushnet 2015). As we will show, however, the attack on horizontal checks can involve a variety of other institutions as well, from ombudsmen and whistleblower laws to central banks and anti-corruption agencies. Ginsburg and Huq (2018) note that such checks extend to the administrative rule of law as well: the presumption that bureaucratic actors will act in accordance with statute and not at the political and personal whim of an autocratic executive.

To sum up, we define backsliding as the result of the purposeful effort of autocrats, who come to power through electoral means, to undermine the three constitutive elements of democracy just outlined. Such regress may take place *within* regimes that remain democratic – a process we label *erosion* – or it can result in regress to authoritarian rule, or *reversion*. Countries that experience erosion remain democratic, but the integrity of the electoral system, the protection of political rights and civil liberties, and horizontal checks are all made weaker as a result of executive action. Backsliding results in reversion when autocrats pursue authoritarian projects that ultimately undermine core democratic institutions altogether, including most notably the bedrock of free and fair elections.

1.2 Toward a Theory of Backsliding

We see backsliding as a complex causal process that we break into three broad steps, although they may overlap in any given case. Our starting point is political polarization, which increases the risk of incumbent parties moving toward extremes or new, anti-system parties gaining traction (Section 2). The second step is that autocrats and their parties exploit polarization to gain executive office and legislative majorities. The electoral victory of the autocrat, combined with control over the legislature, provides the institutional foundation for backsliding (Section 3). Finally, we emphasize that the governing strategies of backsliding autocrats are typically incremental rather than frontal, involving gradual assaults on rights, horizontal checks and the electoral system (Section 4); as we will show, the very incrementalism of the process has a causal effect. Figure 1 provides a schematic guide.

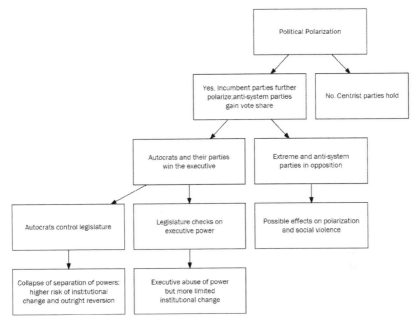

Figure 1: Theoretical Framework.

Our theoretical approach draws on two traditions that have structured the literature. On the one hand, we draw on demand-side theories emphasizing how underlying social cleavages and regime dysfunction can create a market for antidemocratic political appeals. Grievances driven by economic stagnation and/or high inequality have figured prominently in recent analyses (Haggard & Kaufman 1995; Przeworski et al. 2000; Boix 2003; Acemoglu & Robinson 2005; Haggard & Kaufman 2016). However, it is increasingly clear that ethnic, racial, and religious cleavages and fissures between cosmopolitan and nationalist worldviews can be equally, if not more potent, sources of mass polarization (e.g., Mudde & Kaltwasser 2017; Norris & Inglehart 2018).

At the same time, we also build on the seminal work of Linz, Stepan and Valenzuela (1978) on democratic failures in interwar Europe, a tradition that emphasizes elite as well as mass polarization and the failure of political elites and institutions to prevent the emergence and ascent of extremists (Capoccia 2005; Ziblatt 2017). This tradition is alive and well in current discussions of the backsliding process (Levitsky & Ziblatt 2018).

These two strands can be joined by focusing on *political* polarization: the process through which political elites and mass publics become increasingly divided over public policy, ideology and ultimately partisan attachments (Carothers & O'Donohue 2019; McCarty 2019, 8–9). In extremis, crosscutting cleavages are submerged into a single, reinforcing dimension that pits "us" against "them" on a range of issues (McCoy, Rahman & Somer 2018, 18); polarization can become an issue of affect and even identity (Iyengar & Westwood 2015).

Political polarization has a number of adverse effects. It reduces support for centrist political forces and, as a result, opens the door for autocratic electoral appeals. Autocrats make their substantive pitches on a number of grounds that run from ethnonationalism on the right to redistributive class appeals on the left. But these appeals share a number of political commonalities: a celebration of the majoritarian interests of "the people," a disdain for liberal democracy and the procedural rules of the game; denial of the legitimacy of opponents; a willingness to curtail civil liberties; and toleration or even encouragement of violence. The chances of backsliding increase when the center does not hold – when support erodes for political leaders and parties willing and able to resist such appeals.

A second step in the causal chain takes us from polarization to the assumption of power and its exercise. The emergence of antidemocratic parties exerts a pull on existing parties and can thus undermine their ability to act as checks; the latter may even become "complicit backsliders" as a result of electoral concerns. Even in opposition, polarizing leaders and parties can weaken support for democracy and incite social violence.

Nonetheless, backsliding as we define it is ultimately the result of the actions of autocrats who gain executive office and control over the legislature. Holding executive authority is important because of the diverse powers that typically attach to heads of government; there is much damage that executives can do on their own. But backsliding executives will be unable to undertake crucial changes of laws and institutions in the absence of a compliant legislature. For this reason, we place special emphasis on the autocrat's control of legislative majorities, either through a ruling party or in coalition.

Domination of the legislature can contribute to the collapse of the separation of powers by eliminating the legislature as a source of oversight and expanding the discretion of the executive. As we will see, moreover, "captive" legislatures do much more. They rewrite laws surrounding the judiciary, approve executive appointments and pass laws that can erode rights, including freedom of the press. They can even undermine the integrity of the electoral system itself. If control of the legislature is not a *sufficient* condition for the concentration of executive power, it certainly appears *necessary*.

In the third step, we document the causal effects of the incremental nature of the process, what Przeworski (2019) calls "stealth." Executives test normative limits one initiative at a time, with each derogation making subsequent steps easier to pursue (Scheppele 2013). At the broadest level, these steps aim at removing horizontal checks on executive discretion, collapsing the separation of powers. Curtailing the independence of the judiciary and civil service is a key element of the backsliding process, but it also has instrumental value. Autocrats can then test limits by attacking the rights and liberties of opponents. We pay particular attention to attacks on the core rights that are crucial for the functioning of democracy: speech, including freedom of the media, assembly and association. Executives may also reshape voting laws, undermine independent monitoring of elections, and attack opposition parties and civil society groups outright in order to minimize the risks of electoral defeat. As we will show, these steps are typically a prelude to outright reversion to authoritarian rule.

Incrementalism not only has causal effect through institutional and legal changes; we argue it also has social psychological effects. Legally ambiguous steps – especially ones which enjoy popular support – have a disorienting effect on publics, which frequently cannot see that backsliding is taking place until it is too late to respond. Purposeful obfuscation and control of information compounds these difficulties. Initial assaults on horizontal checks, rights and the integrity of the electoral system can easily compound into self-reinforcing cycles, both through the additional powers executives gain and through the disorganization of oppositions and publics.

1.3 Cognate Routes to Democratic Decay

Before diving more deeply into measurement issues, it is worth highlighting a number of other cognate routes through which democracy might weaken and situating those routes vis-à-vis our analysis of backsliding. First, backsliding might arise as a result of defensive strategies on the part of committed democratic governments: efforts to *protect* democracy from the threat of antidemocratic opponents. Such efforts can include curbing (de jure or de facto) the political and civil rights of extremist citizens, including the outlawing of extremist and antidemocratic parties. Cappocia (2005) has shown that such derogations were not uncommon among democracies in the interwar period, including in Czechoslovakia and Finland.

We do not rule out this possibility in current times. Democracies have always grappled with how to balance liberties with appropriate constraints, and particularly during crises: the rise of violent domestic challengers and insurgencies; war; economic crises; and transnational environmental or health challenges such as the

COVID-19 pandemic. We return to this issue briefly in the Conclusion but find that most such justifications in the cases we analyze are disingenuous, including those undertaken in response to the global pandemic of 2020.

In addition to being undermined by executive aggrandizement, democracy could also be undermined by central government weakness: the inability or unwillingness of the center to curb subnational derogations of democratic rule (O'Donnell 2004; Gibson 2012; Mickey, Levitsky & Way 2017; Snyder 2019). This might occur because politicians at the center have political incentives to tolerate abuses by subnational governments or because they simply lack the capacity to control them. In extremis, governments may effectively cede territory to warlords, local autocrats, bosses and *caciques*, or criminal gangs. Such collapses of state authority are clearly more likely among the very poorest countries – so-called failed states – and would therefore not be germane to the cases of interest to us. However, a number of middle-income Latin American countries – Mexico, Colombia and several Central American governments – as well as the Philippines and South Africa raise the issue of subnational authoritarianism as a possible causal path to backsliding.

Finally, we take note of interesting work that suggests that the main challenges to democracy might come not from the actions of political elites but from collusion between political and economic elites and large-scale corruption (Winter 2011; Magyar 2016 on Hungary; Mayer 2017 and Lessig 2018 on the United States). We can imagine a democratic political system in which there are free and fair elections, at least some horizontal checks on executive discretion, and protection of political and civil liberties but also in which executives are accountable not to voters but to oligarchs (Winter 2011). We are reluctant to define backsliding – a fundamentally political process – in these terms alone. Moreover, in our view these oligarchic tendencies reflect decline in institutional dimensions of democratic rule, most notably in checks on the executive and rule of law. However, we are sympathetic to the idea that backsliding may reflect the fusion of autocratic political power to the interests of economic elites; we return to this theme throughout by considering the role that corruption plays in the backsliding process.

1.4 Measurement: Gauging the Extent of Backsliding and Selecting Cases

Turning to issues of measurement, we have the benefit of several recent studies that have outlined the terrain (Lust & Waldner 2015, 2018; Lueders & Lust 2018), which clearly requires continuous rather than dichotomous measures. Table 1 gives an empirical overview of the extent of backsliding in the world

Table 1: Measuring Democratic Regress

Source	Definition	Backsliding
Economist Intelligence Unit Index (2018) 82 countries, 2006–2018.	Distinguishes between full democracies, flawed democracies, hybrid regimes, and authoritarian regimes. Scores based on civil liberties, political culture, participation, government function, electoral process, and pluralism.	Among "full" and "flawed" democracies (n=82): • Declines within democracy: 43% (35 cases) • Decline below democratic threshold: 11% (9 cases)
Freedom House, *Freedom in the World* (2018) 143 countries, 2006-2018.	Overall ratings averaged from separate civil and political rights scores ranging from 1 (most extensive protection of rights) to 7 (least protection); cases divided into "free," "partly free" and "not free."	Among countries rated "free" in 2006 (n=85): • 13% (11 cases) declined within category Among countries rated "free" or "partly free" (n=143) • 22% (31 cases) decline within category • 6% (8 cases) decline to "not free"
Polity2 95 countries, 2006-2017.	Scores capture regime authority spectrum on a 21-point scale ranging from -10 to +10; regimes divided into democracies, anocracies and autocracies.	Among all democracies (n=95): • 7% (7 cases) declined within democracy • 9% (9 cases) fell below the democratic threshold

Table 1: (cont.)

Source	Definition	Backsliding
	Studies Using V–Dem data	
Mechkova, Lührmann, and Lindberg (2017), using regime classification of Lührmann, Lindberg and Tannenberg (2018). 92 countries, 2006-2016.	Electoral democracy: free and fair elections and minimal institutional prerequisites. Liberal democracy: criteria for electoral democracy *plus* legislative and judicial oversight and rule of law.	Among "Liberal Democracies" and "Electoral Democracies" (n=92): • 14% (13 cases) declined while remaining democratic. • 11% (10 cases) decline below democratic threshold.
Mainwaring and Bizzarro (2019), using regime classification of Lührmann, Lindberg and Tannenberg (2018). 91 "Third Wave" democracies, 1974-2017.	Transitions include all changes to Electoral Democracy; Liberal Democracy Index (LDI) used to measure changes in level of democracy.	Among "Third Wave" democracies (n=91): • 5% (4 cases) begin at high LDI levels • 2% (2 cases) experience erosion while remaining democratic; • 37% (34 cases) break down; • 31% (28 cases) stagnate at low levels (mean LDI 0.5) • 25% (23 cases) improve on LDI
Haggard and Kaufman 1974–2017, 103 countries; 2006–2017, 95 countries.	Democratic regimes score at least .5 on the EDI index for at least 8 years. Backsliding is indicated by statistically significant decline in the peak LDI score.	1974 – 2017: • 28% (29 cases) experience significant decline from peak 2006-2017: • 19% (18 cases) experience significant decline from peak

Note: a full description of all variables and methods for deriving our codings is contained in the Appendix.

using four of these measures: from the Economist Intelligence Unit (EIU 2020); Freedom House (2020); the Polity project (Marshall, Gurr & Jaggers 2019); and V-Dem (Coppedge et al. 2019). The upper half of the table considers the so-called democratic recession that is typically dated to the mid-2000s (2006 through 2017 or 2018, depending on indicator; see the contrasting views of Diamond 2015; Levitsky and Way 2015). The second half of the table looks at several studies using V-Dem data, both for the more recent period and for the entire Third Wave, including our favored measure.

It is important to underscore that, although these measures are correlated, they ultimately rest on subtly different definitions of democracy and generate somewhat different overall assessments as well as cases. These differences are dissected in more detail in the online Appendix, but the EIU, Polity and V-Dem datasets might be considered "omnibus" measures seeking to capture all of the defining features of democratic rule, while the Freedom House focuses more narrowly on one crucial component of democracy: the protection of political and civil liberties.

All of the studies we survey distinguish between higher- and lower-quality democracies, and it is possible to trace democratic deterioration both within and across each of these categories. For our purposes, however, it is sufficient to focus on declines that occur *within* democratic regimes (of both high and low quality) and those that end in a *reversion* to authoritarianism. Assessments of decline within democratic regimes varied widely across the datasets. During the "democratic recession" period beginning in 2006, democracies experiencing such declines ranged from 43 percent in the EIU data to only 7 percent using Polity. There was less variation in the percentage of democratic breakdowns during this period. Of the Freedom House cases, 6 percent declined to "not free," while breakdowns registered by EIU, Polity, and Mechkova, Lührmann, and Lindberg (2017) ranged from 9 to 11 percent of all the cases. With the exception of Polity, declines within democracies outnumbered full breakdowns, and, although it is not shown in Table 1, the breakdowns generally occurred among the weaker democratic regimes. We show similar results in Table 2 as well as in our analysis of the backsliding process in Section 4.

Unlike these other datasets, Mainwaring and Bizzarro (2019) focus exclusively on the fate of ninety-one "Third Wave" democracies from 1974 and 2017. Their conclusions are not encouraging. More than two-thirds (68 percent) of these regimes either stagnated at very low levels or broke down entirely. In contrast to the other measures, which capture democratic erosion among more established democracies, Mainwaring and Bizzarro find only two such cases among the new democracies (Ecuador and Poland); a core finding of their study is that erosion is not a stable equilibrium but slides either into full breakdown or a restoration of democracy.

Our preferred measure, like Mainwaring and Bizzarro (2019) and Mechkova et al. (2017), deploys V-Dem data. Our analysis of this data covers the period from 1974 through 2017, but we show results for the democratic deficit period as well. Our standard for defining democracy is relatively demanding. A country must experience at least eight consecutive years with a score of at least 0.5 on the V-Dem Electoral Democracy (EDI) index, which puts particular weight on what might be called "the basics": free, fair and competitive elections with freedom for political and civil society organizations to operate.

The onset of a backsliding episode, however, is marked by a statistically significant decline from a country's peak score on the V-Dem *Liberal* Democracy Index (LDI). In addition to the components of the EDI, the LDI also considers civil liberties, the rule of law, and effective checks and balances, including an independent judiciary; see the online Appendix for a full explanation of the coding. The motivation for using the LDI to capture backsliding is our belief that derogations from democratic rule do not necessarily arise from direct assaults on the integrity of the electoral system or the protection of basic rights to association. We want a more nuanced indicator to capture horizontal checks and the protection of civil liberties as well. In addition to capturing erosion, this measure permits us to identify outright reversion as well: any case of a decline below 0.5 in the EDI is identified as a regime change.

This method generated an initial list of twenty-nine backsliding cases. As a validity check, however, we undertook a second step: to compare our list of cases with the other datasets outlined in Table 1 as well as the other uses of V-Dem there. Those that are identified as eroding or reverting to authoritarian rule by at least two other measures are included in our list of backsliding cases in Table 2; others were eliminated even though they constitute important marginal cases, some clearly showing signs of backsliding. For those included cases, we note whether and when they underwent erosion – a decline that stops short of an outright regime change – or whether they experienced a full reversion to authoritarian rule.[2]

Our methodological approach selects on the dependent variable, considering these backsliding cases as our sample. We frame our analysis of the backsliding cases with comparative reference to regional benchmarks. However, our primary interest is in exploring the plausibility of the postulated causal mechanisms we have identified, an analytic focus for which this

---

[2] The V-Dem data initially used to select cases was v.8 of the data set, which went through 2017. We subsequently coded whether the backsliding episode continued into 2018–2019 or ended; see the online Appendix for more detail on coding rules.

Table 2: Cases and Coding (Erosion and Reversion)

Country	Coding
Bolivia 2007-2019	*Erosion* from electoral democracy, 2007.
Brazil 2016-19	*Erosion* from liberal democracy. 2016.
The Dominican Republic 2014-2018	*Erosion* from electoral democracy, 2014.
Ecuador 2009-2017	*Erosion* from electoral democracy, 2009.
Greece 2017-2019	*Erosion* from liberal democracy, 2017.
Hungary 2011-2019	*Erosion* from liberal democracy, 2011.
Macedonia 2010-2016	*Erosion* from electoral democracy 2010, *reversion* 2012.
Nicaragua 2005-2019	*Erosion* from electoral democracy 2005; *reversion* 2008.
Poland 2016-2019	*Erosion* from liberal democracy, 2016.
Russia 2000-2019	*Reversion* from electoral democracy 2000.
Serbia 2013-2019	*Erosion* from electoral democracy 2013, *reversion* 2017.
Turkey 2010-2019	*Erosion* from electoral democracy 2010, *reversion* 2014.
Ukraine 2010-2018	*Erosion* from electoral democracy 2010, *reversion* 2014.
United States 2016-2019	*Erosion* from liberal democracy 2016.
Venezuela 1998-2019	*Erosion* from electoral democracy 1998; *reversion* 2006.
Zambia 2016-2019	*Reversion* from electoral democracy 2016

sort of large-N qualitative analysis is appropriate (Haggard & Kaufman 2016). In the following sections we draw on illustrative examples, based on more detailed causal process observations contained in the online Appendix case studies. We begin our narrative with a consideration of the effects of polarization in Section 2.

2 Social and Political Origins of Backsliding: The Role of Polarization

In this section we explore how polarization feeds into the backsliding process. Polarization is the *process* through which political elites and publics become increasingly divided over public policy, ideology and ultimately partisan attachments (McCarty 2019, 8–9). This may happen because voters sort themselves into political parties, social groups or "tribes" that are more homogenous. Such sorting does not necessarily mean a move toward extremes, but it nonetheless results in sharper partisan and group differences. Yet such political and social division can also arise from divisions among both elites and mass publics that pull them – centripetally – toward extremes. Previously cross-cutting cleavages can submerge into a single, reinforcing dimension that pits "Us" against "Them" on a range of key issues (McCoy, Rahman & Somer 2018), a phenomenon known as negative partisanship. Polarization becomes an issue of affect and even identity (Iyengar & Westwood 2015).

Political scientists have spilled significant ink on whether polarization is driven by elites or mass publics and, of course, on what the underlying causal forces are that generate it. We consider measures of polarization at the level of both elites and voters and focus particular attention both in this section and the next on how polarization manifests itself in the electoral arena. Such political polarization sets the stage for backsliding in three interrelated ways: through its effect on the functioning of government and resulting disaffection and distrust of democracy; through the appeal of anti-system leaders, parties and social movements; and through the willingness of both elites and publics in polarized settings to tolerate derogations from democracy. We pay particular attention to populist political appeals that embody a majoritarian conception of democracy: one in which the will of "the people" is believed to override the procedural constaints of democratic rule.

Given the causal weight we place on these processes, we need to consider whether the observed increase in political polarization arises from some underlying cause. As we showed in Section 1, the majority of backsliding episodes in our sample occurred in the aftermath of the Global Financial Crisis that erupted in 2008, and some – such as Greece – quite obviously emanated from it. A number of earlier episodes of backsliding occurred in the aftermath of crises as well, most notably in Venezuela and Russia. Yet economic factors may not operate to generate polarization only in crisis settings. Przeworski (2019, chapter 6), for example, identifies a number of long-run developments in the advanced industrial states that might contribute to polarization including stagnant wage growth and the near-global trend toward increasing inequality (McCarty, Poole & Rosenthal

2016); inequality has even been implicated – at least in theory – with regime change (Boix 2003; Acemoglu & Robinson 2006; but see Haggard & Kaufman 2016). And these developments in turn have deeper causal roots, including increasing economic integration and exposure to trade and skill-biased, labor-displacing technological change (Autor et al. 2017).

Polarization also arises around racial and ethnic divisions, with immigration a particular point of contention in Europe and the United States (Abrajano & Hajnal 2017). Cultural differences between cosmopolitan and nationalist, religious and secular worldviews have also played a role in a number of cases in our sample, evident in the rise of Euroskeptic parties on both the left and right in Europe (eg. Norris & Inglehart 2018; Mudde & Kaltwasser 2017)

Our intuition from the cases is that it is hard to trace political polarization back to any single taproot. Precisely because polarization subsumes a variety of previously overlapping divisions, countries polarize in distinctive ways. Although we explore the underlying sources of polarization in the cases that follow and in the online Appendix, we focus particular attention on the political risks such divisions pose once unleashed.

We begin by examining the political consequences of polarization in more detail. We use some simple metrics to demonstrate the extent of both elite and mass polarization in our cases and the precise nature of the substantive appeals used by autocrats and their parties. We then take a deeper dive into several exemplary but otherwise diverse cases – Brazil, Poland and the United States – showing the mechanisms through polarization contributes to the appeal of autocrats. We close with an overview of the electoral circumstances under which the autocratic politicians in our sample actually gained executive office, noting that, despite majoritarian appeals, they frequently come to office with only pluralities of electoral support.

2.1 The Effects of Polarization

Although there is substantial debate over the relative weight of elite and mass public polarization (McCarty 2019, 22–68), we pose the causal question in a general way that is applicable to both processes. Why might polarization be conducive to the rise of autocrats and public tolerance for derogations from democratic rule? And how might autocrats themselves stoke divisions in order to solidify their hold on power?

A first reason focuses on performance. Social perceptions of political competitors in stark, binary terms – as the "other" – reduce incentives for the kinds of policy compromises required for effective democratic governance. Where opposing parties are polarized, government is less likely to function efficiently and more likely to witness either stalemates or swings between policy extremes. The result is an increase in disaffection and distrust of institutions more generally. Elites and publics are more likely to see democracy itself – as opposed to any particular incumbent – as dysfunctional. As recent studies of the advanced industrial states have shown, support for democracy itself can erode (Armingeon & Guthman 2014; Mounk 2018).

Second, by definition polarization is a process in which both elites and publics become more divided. While this may not necessarily entail a move toward political extremes, it quite frequently has. As divisions among political contenders sharpen and widen, polarization enhances the likelihood that "anti-system" (Sartori 1966) social movements and parties gain footholds in the political system.

Finally, the recasting of social competition into stark we/they binaries is associated with a particularly majoritarian conception of democratic rule, often identified with populism. The very concept of populism is widely con-tested, and contemporary populism is clearly protean. It ranges from far-right nationalists and even fascists to left-wing variants promising radical economic redistribution (see Mudde & Kaltwasser 2017 for an overview). However, students of populism have noted common *political* threads in populist discourse that are highly germane to an understanding of backsliding regardless of the substantive demands populists make. Populist movements not only align "the people" or the nation against prevailing elites but claim connection to a Rousseuvian "general will," typically rooted in the nation or "the people." Autocrats instantiate this general will and promise an unmediated relationship with their followers. Above all, they promise a majoritarian approach to dem-ocracy unfettered by checks on executive discretion or procedural niceties. As a number of studies of populism have noted, these movements are hostile to liberal conceptions of democracy – on which our analytic framework is ultim-ately based – even if they do not openly embrace dictatorial rule (from different perspectives, Weyland 2001; Mudde & Rovira Kaltwasser 2017; Eatwell and Goodwin 2018; Eichengreen 2018; Kenny 2019; Urbinati 2019).

Although the appeals of autocrats may not be openly authoritarian, they nonetheless have the effect of "disfiguring" democratic rule, as Urbinati (2019, 3–16) puts it. In an important theoretical contribution, Svolik (2018) shows how voters in polarized political systems are more likely to acquiesce to derogations from democratic procedures precisely because they see the oppos-ition as unacceptable or even threatening and dangerous (see also experimental results to this effect in Graham & Svolik 2019). Majoritarian appeals and an emphasis on threats not only affect formal political processes, they can instigate violence and vigilantism in civil society. Elite and mass tolerance for departures from democratic "rules of the game" goes directly to process of backsliding: the erosion of horizontal checks, weakening protection for political rights and civil liberties, and ultimately meddling in elections themselves.

As Levitsky and Ziblatt (2018) argue, moreover, democracy rests not only on formal institutions and rules but on deeper normative restraints as well: the willingness to underutilize the formal powers of office and to accept the necessity of compromise. Polarization reduces the political incentives to abide by these normative guardrails. Politics becomes more like a security dilemma, in which stakes are raised dramatically by the self-fulfilling prophecy that winners will fundamentally tilt the playing field in their favor (Haggard & Kaufman 2016, 226–288; Przeworski 2019, 164–171). As Lenin put it in a concise formulation, politics is reduced to the question of "who whom" (кто-кого). Who will dominate, and who will be sidelined, even permanently?

2.2 Political Polarization: An Empirical Overview

Measuring polarization within a single country is contentious; it is even more difficult to capture the extent of polarization across diverse countries in a uniform way. We undertake the task in two steps, drawing on several V-Dem indicators to provide a sense of the extent of polarization in our cases; and then turning to the nature of the substantive appeals autocrats and their political machines and movements bring to the fore.

2.2.1 The Extent of Elite and Mass Polarization

We draw first on four indicators from the V-Dem dataset – based on expert codings – that measure aggregate trends in both elite and mass polarization; a more detailed explanation of the variables is contained in the online Appendix. The first two of these capture strains at the elite level and with respect to parties; the second two capture mass sentiment and developments in civil society.

- The extent to which political elites acknowledge and respect counterarguments, scored from 0 (no counterarguments allowed) to 4 (elites generally respect and value counterarguments)
- The frequency of hate speech in the rhetoric of the political parties: scored from 0 (extremely often) to 3 or 4 (rarely or almost never).
- Polarization of society, ranging from serious differences of opinion on all key political issues (scored as 0) to limited or no major differences (scored as 3 or 4).
- The extent of anti-system civil society and social movements, scored from minimal (0) to 3 or 4 (posing substantial or high-level threats to the system);

note that this is one indicator in which higher scores reflect more rather than less polarization.

Table 3 summarizes polarization on each of these measures both prior to and following the onset of the backsliding episode. The first column considers the level of polarization in the country in question, benchmarking it against regional comparators; were the backsliding cases more polarized than the regional averages?[3] The second and third columns consider whether there was a statistically significant increase in polarization during two time frames. The first considers the period from t-10 through the first several years of the backsliding episode (until t+2); this measure is designed to capture antecedent conditions and a period that typically corresponds with the transition to new governments. The last column reports whether there was a statistically significant increase in polarization during the backsliding episode itself, on the hypothesis that autocrats not only exploit polarization but aggravate it once in office.

The results are easily summarized. First, the overwhelming majority of our cases show a higher level of polarization than their counterparts, and nine countries – Ecuador, Hungary, North Macedonia, Poland, Serbia, Turkey, Ukraine, the USA, Zambia – are more polarized than the benchmark countries on all four of the V-Dem measures. The only country that was not more polarized on any of the four measures was the Dominican Republic, where the backsliding episode itself was comparatively limited and brief. While the share of countries experiencing increases in polarization is somewhat less than those that show higher levels of polarization, the roll call nonetheless includes a large majority of the cases. Moreover, every single case showed an increase on at least one of the measures of polarization in the run-up to the backsliding episode.

The backsliding period itself shows somewhat more mixed results; this is in part because, in many of our cases, polarization had already increased to very high levels by the time autocrats came to power. Nonetheless, it is worth highlighting a particular dynamic which occurred in a number of the left-populist Latin American cases in particular. Backsliding incumbents push forward a polarizing political and policy agenda, steamrolling over restraints. But this behavior stimulated a counterreaction among mass publics and civil society, including through contentious politics. In 75 percent of our cases, we see an increase in anti-system movements in civil society during the backsliding period. Some of these involved groups associated with the regime, including

---

[3] A country is coded as "more polarized" if it differed from the regional benchmark in any year in the t-10 to t-1 period. Latin American cases are compared to Latin American averages, Greece and the Eastern European cases, Turkey, Russia and Ukraine are compared to Western Europe and Zambia to Mauritius, the country in Africa with one of the longest democratic records.

Table 3: Polarization in Backsliding Countries

	Countries more polarized than benchmarks (*t-10* to *t+2*)	Countries with an increase in polarization (*t-10* to *t+2*)	Countries with an increase in polarization (*t* to end of episode or 2019)
		Elite polarization	
Respect counterarguments	Bolivia, Brazil, Ecuador, Nicaragua, Venezuela, Hungary, Macedonia, Poland, Russia, Serbia, Turkey, Ukraine, US, Zambia	Bolivia, Brazil, Nicaragua, Venezuela, Greece, Hungary, Macedonia, Poland, Russia, Serbia, Turkey, US, Zambia	Bolivia, Brazil, DR, Nicaragua, Venezuela, Hungary, Russia, Turkey, US
	14/16, 87.5%	13/16, 81.25%	9/16, 56.25%
Political parties hate speech	Brazil, Ecuador, Venezuela, Greece, Hungary, Macedonia, Poland, Russia, Serbia, Turkey, Ukraine, US, Zambia	Brazil, Dominican Republic, Nicaragua, Greece, Hungary, Macedonia, Poland, Serbia, Turkey, Ukraine, US, Zambia	Bolivia, Brazil, Dominican Republic, Nicaragua, Venezuela, Hungary, Russia, Turkey, Ukraine
	13/16, 81.25%	12/15, 80% NA: Venezuela	9/16, 56.25%

Table 3: (cont.)

	Countries more polarized than benchmarks (t-10 to t+2)	Countries with an increase in polarization (t-10 to t+2)	Countries with an increase in polarization (t to end of episode or 2019)
		Mass polarization and civil society	
Polarization of society	Bolivia, Brazil, Ecuador, Venezuela, Greece, Hungary, Macedonia, Poland, Serbia, Turkey, Ukraine, US, Zambia	Bolivia, Brazil, Ecuador, Greece, Hungary, Macedonia, Poland, Turkey, Ukraine, US, Zambia	Bolivia, Brazil, Dominican Republic, Nicaragua, Venezuela, Poland, Turkey, Ukraine
	13/15, 86.6% NA: Russia	11/15, 73.3% NA: Venezuela	8/16, 50%
CSO Anti-system movements	Bolivia, Brazil, Ecuador, Venezuela, Greece, Hungary, Macedonia, Poland, Russia, Serbia, Turkey, Ukraine, US, Zambia	Bolivia, Brazil, Ecuador, Venezuela, Greece, Hungary, Macedonia, Poland, Ukraine, US, Zambia	Bolivia, Brazil, Dominican Republic, Nicaragua, Venezuela, Macedonia, Poland, Russia, Turkey, Ukraine, US, Zambia
	14/16, 87.5%	11/16, 68.75%	12/16, 75%

vigilantes and even death squads, but some were seeking to mobilize publics in opposition. We will see these dynamics in more detail when we consider the cases of Venezuela, Bolivia and Ecuador in the next section.

2.2.2 The Politics of Polarization

What are the dominant political and social dimensions along which elites and mass publics divide in the backsliding countries? As can be seen, the cases are highly diverse, ranging from the United States to upper- and middle-income countries on the European periphery to poorer countries such as Bolivia, Ecuador and Zambia. We would not necessarily expect all cases to divide in similar ways. We focus on what might be called the "backsliding elections" in which autocrats come to office, providing data on three features of these crucial junctures: the autocrats' vote share; whether there is evidence of partisan polarization and a weakening of incumbent and centrist parties; and the political and policy cleavages that autocrats and their parties sought to exploit.

A first point to note is the number of cases in which the backsliding episode was preceded by significant decline in the vote shares of previously dominant parties (for details on each case, see the online Appendix; see also Przeworski 2019, chapter 5; and Vachudova 2020 on the European cases). Disaffection with the political status quo in these countries was clearly high. In some cases the established party system collapsed altogether, creating the space for new entrants. This was true in Bolivia, Ecuador, Greece, Venezuela and Zambia, most of which experienced significant financial crises prior to the onset of backsliding.

A number of other cases saw changes in the leadership or orientation of *existing* parties that shifted them toward extremes, typically in the context of the emergence of even more radical challengers, parties or social movements on the ideological fringes of the system. This pattern was visible in some of the cases cited earlier – for example, with respect to New Democracy in Greece – but is particularly clear in the United States, Hungary and Poland. In the United States, mainstream Republican candidates were eviscerated in the primaries by Donald Trump's populist campaign, causing power within the party to subsequently shift in Trump's direction. Hungary and Poland saw more continuous leadership but also saw the manifestos of major parties shift right as a result of the changing views of dominant incumbents.

In four cases – the Dominican Republic, Nicaragua, Turkey and Russia – the party system did not polarize in any of the ways just described. But Turkey, Russia and Nicaragua conform to the generalization in important respects. In Turkey, Erdoğan shifted the AKP toward more open Islamist appeals following his second electoral victory in 2007, and polarization increased accordingly. In Russia, the party system was already fragmented at the end of the Yeltsin era, with new parties entering the scene in the 1999 Duma elections. However, Putin's election to a powerful presidency in 2000 allowed him to dominate United Russia, which quickly became the instrument of the president in the legislature. And in Nicaragua, Daniel Ortega returned to power due to a fissure within the Liberal Party that opened the door to the Sandinistas, the principle protagonist of the country's civil war.

What is the nature of the cleavages around which polarization occurs? What types of appeals did these backsliding candidates and parties make? A handful appear relatively centrist in their initial campaigns. This is true in Serbia, Turkey and Zambia, although in all three of these cases polarizing appeals become more apparent over time. In the others, polarization was driven either from the populist right or the left, with Brazil and the United States representing more complex hybrids of economic, racial/ethnic and cultural appeals. The Dominican Republic is the only case in which the party system doesn't undergo a significant polarization, and, as noted, it experienced a relatively limited and brief backsliding episode.

In virtually all of the European cases in the sample, with the exception of Greece, polarization centers on right-nationalist appeals on the one hand – with religion often playing an underappreciated role – and more cosmopolitan forces on both the left and right with respect to economic issues (Vachudova 2020). These divisions often had deep historical roots, in some cases dating to the rise of fascism in the interwar period. In the former socialist cases, these cleavages also reflected resentments that arose around the political and social upheavals associated with the transition from communist rule, for example with respect to less educated and more rural voters. This is true of Russia and Hungary, pioneers in the backsliding process, as well as Poland, Ukraine and the Balkan cases (represented in our sample by North Macedonia and Serbia, but with Croatia as a marginal case as well). In a somewhat different context, Turkish backsliding also built on appeals to religious voters in less-favored regions of the country.

A final overlay in these European cases is the rise of anti-immigrant sentiment, peaking during the Syrian refugee crisis of 2015–2016 but in some cases (such as North Macedonia) having more local origins. Countries differed dramatically in the extent to which they were directly affected by the crisis, with Greece and particularly Turkey being among the most affected in all of Europe. But even in those where absorption of refugees was limited, populists adopted a racialized discourse on them; this was true in Hungary and Poland in particular.

It is worth underscoring that while economic crises played some role in subsequent polarization, most notably in Russia, others do not show unusual economic stress. Some – most notably Poland – had strong growth prior to the onset of the backsliding episode. Yet this does not rule out the possibility that differential life chances and rising inequality played a role in stoking social resentments.

Table 4: Popular Vote Share of Autocrat, Party Polarization, Political Appeals

	Popular vote share of autocrat (presidential or parliamentary)	Party polarization	Political Appeals of Autocrat
Bolivia 2007-2019	53.7% (presidential)	Traditional parties collapse in 2000s; extensive grass roots mobilization and rise of MAS-IPSP	Morales appeals to indigenous peoples, strong left-populist program.
Brazil 2016-2019	1st round: 46% 2nd round 55.1% (presidential)	Rise of new right movements; establshed parties–PT, PSDB and PMDB—see largest defeats ever.	Bolsonaro runs on right populist platform: traditional religious values (targeting women, gays); strongly anti-left; expresses nostalgia for military rule.
Dominican Republic 2014-2018	51.2% (presidential)	PLD continues to dominate presidential voting	Competing politicians exploit prejudices toward Dominico-Haitians and Haitian immigrants by challenging citizenship rights.

Table 4: (cont.)

	Popular vote share of autocrat (presidential or parliamentary)	Party polarization	Political Appeals of Autocrat
Ecuador 2009-2017	Rafael Correa, October 2006	1st round: 22.8% 2nd round: 56.7% (presidential)	Sharp decline in vote share of traditional parties; rise of socialist PAIS (2006)	Correa runs strongly anti-elite campaign, with allies in indigenous, feminist, and environmentalist social movements. Left-populist program.
Greece 2017-2019	Alexis Tsipras (Syriza), January 2015	36.3% (parliamentary)	Vote share of dominant parties (PASOK and New Democracy) collapse after the Global Financial Crisis. Rise of populist (ANEL) and far right (Golden Dawn) parties. Populist turn by New Democracy.	Syriza rejects terms of European bailout and continuing austerity. Left-populist program although moderated in office.
Hungary 2010-2019	Orbán (FIDESZ), 2010	53.5% (parliamentary, constituency seats), 52.7% (list seats)	Socialist Party sees collapse of support. Orbán and FIDESZ move right. Rise of far-right Jobbik.	Fidesz capitalizes on insecurities related to market reform, disaffection with incumbents over corruption scandal and aftermath of great recession. But also strong cosmopolitan-nationalist divide.

North Macedonia 2010-2016	Nikola Gruevski (VMRO-DPMNE), July 2006	32.3% (parliamentary)	Two coalitions—VMRO-DPMNE and Social Democratic Coalition—dominate	Right-nationalist VMRO-DPMNE focuses on ethnic Macedonians and identity politics, including vis-à-vis dispute with Greece. Cosmopolitan-nationalist divide.
Nicaragua, 2005-2019	Daniel Ortega, November 2006	38.1%	Anti-Sandinista parties divide (PLC and ALN), creating electoral opening for Sandinistas	Weaker evidence of polarization, but Ortega comes out of hard-left political tradition.
Poland 2016-2019	Jarosław Kaczyński (Peace and Justice Party), 2015	37.6% (parliamentary)	Divisions among traditional left parties during 2000s. Rise of new entrants on the Euroskeptic and nationalist right.	PiS runs relatively moderate campaign but emphasizes Euroskepticism and traditional values, including role of Catholic Church. Cosmopolitan-nationalist divide.

Table 4: (cont.)

	Popular vote share of autocrat (presidential or parliamentary)	Party polarization	Political Appeals of Autocrat
Russia 2000-2019	Vladimir Putin, March 2000	53.0% (presidential)	Fragmentation of party system with new groupings dominating 1999 legislative elections.	Putin offers a broad right-nationalist platform including anti-terrorism (Second Chechen war), the need to strengthen the state, traditional values and restoration of Russia's role as a great power. Cosmopolitan-nationalist divide.
Serbia 2013-2019	[May 2012, Ivica Dačić (Socialist)]; March 2014, Aleksandar Vučić (SNS), March 2014	48.3% (parliamentary, 2014)	Liberal Democratic Party and Democratic Party fail to meet electoral threshold in 2014 and SNS coalition dominates. Rise of right-wing parties in 2016 elections.	SNS makes broadly centrist-reformist appeals (fiscal rectitude, corruption, approach to EU) but shifts on taking office to more nationalist appeals. Cosmopolitan-nationalist divide.

Turkey 2010–2019	Recep Erdoğan (AKP), November 2002	34.3% (parliamentary)	Collapse of DSP-MHP-ANAP coalition opens space for AKP, but no radical or anti-system parties.	AKP runs on moderate, center-right manifesto in 2002 election. Subsequently, Erdoğan moves to more openly Islamist and nationalist appeals in 2007 elections.
Ukraine 2010–2018	Viktor Yanukovych, January-February 2010	36.8% (presidential, first round) 51.8% (second round)	Victory of Party of Regions in 2010 triggers growth of far-right parties, social movements, and Donbass separatists.	Party of Regions is broadly centrist on policy issues, but clear base in Russian-speaking East. Pro-Europe/cosmopolitan-nationalist divide.
United States, 2016–2019	Donald Trump, November 2016	46.1% (presidential, wins via electoral college against 48.2% vote share for Hillary Clinton)	Two-party system, but centrist Republicans lose control of the party to Trump during 2016 primaries.	Strong anti-elite, right-populist and nationalist appeals with a major focus on trade and immigration. Cosmopolitan-nationalist divide.

Table 4: (cont.)

	Popular vote share of autocrat (presidential or parliamentary)	Party polarization	Political Appeals of Autocrat
Venezuela 1998-2019	Hugo Chávez, December 1998 — 56.2% (presidential)	Collapse of traditional two-party system; rise of independents and left parties.	Chávez makes strong left-populist and redistributive appeals.
Zambia 2016-2019	Edgar Lungu, January 2015 — 48.8% (presidential)	Broad umbrella opposition (MMD) collapses, opening the door to return of two dominant regional parties.	2015 and 2016 elections stoke class divisions in the urban centers and copper belt and regional-cum ethnic divisions in the Bemba-speaking North and East and Loze and other ethnic groups in the West and South.

Note: for a full list of party acronyms, see the Appendix.

In the cluster of left-populist cases, by contrast, all had traumatic economic histories running up to the backsliding episodes. Most notable in this regard are Venezuela and Greece. Hugo Chávez represents a style of Latin American populism that can be dated to interwar leaders such as Getúlio Vargas in Brazil, Juan Perón in Argentina and José María Velasco Ibarra in Ecuador. The Syriza party in Greece was subsequently constrained to push through reforms it had initially run against, but it did so in a context roiled by the rise of populist parties on the left and right (ANEL, Golden Dawn) as well as the reorientation of existing parties – most notably New Democracy – in a decidedly more Euroskeptic direction. Economic crises and populist appeals were visible in Bolivia and Ecuador as well, although with the additional twist that these two Latin American cases also had long histories of suppression of the interests of indigenous peoples. Economic populism was in fact driven in large part by social movements – to some extent violent – that sought to bring indigenous people more squarely into the political mainstream.

Finally, we see several cases in which polarization reflects complex and overlapping cleavages. In the United States these include not only the aftermath of the global financial crisis and rising inequality and economic anxiety but the longer-run unraveling of the New Deal coalition and cultural anxieties among middle-aged white men in particular. Immigration became a central issue in the campaign, as it was in a number of European countries as well, from Britain's ongoing Brexit saga to the rise of anti-immigrant parties in France, Germany, Austria, and even the Netherlands and Scandinavia.

To explore these very different ways in which countries can polarize, we consider the cases of Brazil, Poland and the United States. All were coded as liberal democracies presumed immune from serious political risk. Yet all experienced significant political polarization prior to the onset of backsliding.

Brazil shows how economic and political shocks can combine to increase disaffection with incumbent parties and open the door for disruptive outsiders exploiting cultural divisions, including religion. Poland, by contrast, demonstrates that similar developments can emerge in the context of strong economic performance. In the United States, finally, a slow-moving realignment of the party system had been in train over decades, coming together in Trump's highly disruptive majoritarian political campaign in 2016.

2.3 Brazil, 2016–2019

Until a few years prior to the onset of its backsliding episode, Brazil was generally considered exemplary of South America's successful transition to democratic rule. As can be seen in Figure 2 – which goes back ten years before

Political Economy

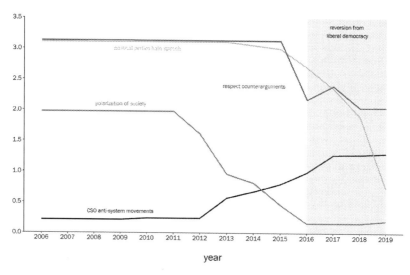

year

Figure 2: Polarization in Brazil, 2006–2019.

the onset of the backsliding episode – measures of polarization showed little change in the second half of the 2000s. However between 2013 and the onset of the backsliding episode in 2016, all four indicators take a significant turn for the worse. The precipitating causes included a deep economic crisis and rising anxiety about public safety (Hunter & Powers 2019). But polarization itself centered on deep divisions over a corruption scandal and the impeachment of the incumbent president. The polarization of elites and the public set the stage for derogations from democratic rule and the election of Jair Bolsonaro, who emerged from the margins of the political system as support for mainstream political parties deteriorated.

The recession that hit Brazil between 2014 and 2016 was the worst in Brazil's history and clearly played a role in growing polarization and disaffection with the government. GDP growth was close to zero in 2014 and declined by almost 8 percent in 2015 and again in 2016, before returning to an anemic 1 percent growth in 2017. Many factors contributed to this crash, including a sharp downturn in commodity prices, but it was exacerbated by the fiscal policies of the Rousseff administration. In the runup to the 2014 presidential election, Rousseff attempted to avert an economic slowdown by running large off-the-books fiscal deficits in 2013 and 2014. But once the elections were safely behind her, she imposed a harsh austerity program in an attempt to correct course. Between January 2014 and its peak in March 2017, the unemployment rate in the country more than doubled from 6.2 to 13.7 percent.

Concurrent with the economic crisis was the rising salience of violent crime, an issue that frequently serves as a justification for extra-democratic measures. In 2017, seventeen Brazilian cities ranked among the fifty most violent cities in the world (Hunter & Power 2019, 73). Indeed the onset of the backsliding episode in Brazil – coming two years before the 2018 election of Bolsonaro – was associated in part with controversial measures taken by the Temer government to grant jurisdiction to the military to prosecute crimes involving civilians.

Yet it was ultimately political and partisan polarization that set the stage for backsliding. In 2013, the country witnessed massive protests around provision of public services, including particularly urban transport, and overspending associated with the World Cup and the Olympics. The protests broadened to focus on a litany of disaffections, including corruption in government, and the 2014 elections were among the most polarized in Brazilian history. The Northeast voted overwhelmingly for the PT and the South supported the opposition candidacy of Aécio Neves, the centrist candidate of the Party of Brazilian Social Democracy (PSDB).

The political waters were roiled further by revelations, first surfacing in 2014, that much of the political and major corporations had been entangled in kick-back and bribery schemes (the so-called "Lava Jato" or "Car Wash" scandal). Federal prosecutors ultimately levied thirty-seven criminal charges against 179 politicians and business leaders. The initial targets were mainly incumbent Labor Party politicians and their allies, who had been in power since 2003. Former president Lula da Silva was imprisoned and barred from running for the presidency in 2018. But the prosecution ultimately touched politicians from across the political spectrum and contributed to growing disaffection with the political class as a whole.

The impeachment of incumbent PT president Dilma Rousseff further polar-ized the political system. Rousseff was charged with violation of federal budgetary laws, not with the Lava Jato corruption that had tainted other politi-cians. But the campaign for her ouster was joined by former allies – including Vice President Michel Temer of the opposition PMDB – who were themselves implicated. The socially conservative and economically right-wing Free Brazil Movement played a role in Rouseff's ouster, particularly through savvy use of social media and the mobilization of mass protest. Embittered supporters of the besieged president characterized the impeachment as a *golpe* against the will of the voters, but the damage to the mainstream parties had been done and cut across the board.

The convergence of these crises contributed to a marked deterioration in the legitimacy of the political system as a whole. Hunter and Power (2019, 74) note that "2015 was an inflection point in Brazilians' support for democracy. The number of respondents who agreed that 'Democracy is preferable to any other system of government' started to fall, while the view that 'For people like me, it doesn't matter whether we have a democratic government or an authoritarian one' began gaining in popularity."

The litany of factors noted here – poor economic performance, declining security, the corruption scandal, and the impeachment – combined in the 2018 elections to yield a striking result: the collapse of support for the two parties – the PT (Labor Party) and the PSDB (Social Democratic Party of Brazil) – that had long been the principal competitors for the presidency and the dramatic rise of Jair Bolsonaro from the fringe of the system. In addition to playing on a series of wedge issues – religion, traditional gender roles and opposition to affirmative action – Bolsonaro's campaign included explicit appeals to authoritarian politics. He spoke nostalgically about the period of military dictatorship, praised autocrats such as Alberto Fujimori of Peru and Augusto Pinochet of Chile, and promised a tough law-and-order campaign that would give police expanded powers to use force against urban crime and drug trafficking. In the first round of presidential voting, he secured a shocking 46 percent of the popular vote before coasting to victory in the second round.

In sum, economic crises played an important role in polarizing the Brazilian public. But the corruption scandal, impeachment and elite polarization immobilized the government, deepening general political disaffection. Although the backsliding episode we identify began before the election of 2018, the implosion of centrist parties opened the space for a populist alternative.

2.4 Poland, 2016–2019

What were the sources of polarization in Poland? The country largely escaped the shock of the Great Recession and recovered more quickly than other countries in the region. There were, to be sure, winners and losers in the transition to the market, and the PiS (Law and Justice Party) appealed to those who were left behind, including in rural areas. As with Trump's followers in the United States, Law and Justice voters were older, more rural and religious, and less well-educated that their Civic Platform counterparts (Szczerbiak 2017). But studies of voting behavior in the 2015 election do not find evidence that individual-level economic factors were a determinant of PiS votes (Markowski 2016).

Nonetheless, we not only find that Poland more polarized than its European counterparts on two of the four measures we use (polarization of society and hate speech); we also see a deterioration in all of the proxies for polarization that we have identified here (Figure 3). What accounts for increasing polarization, and what were its effects?

The sources of polarization can be found to a significant extent on the supply side, in the changing nature of PiS appeals. By 2005, the initial post-transition party system had gone through a realignment. Until that time, two blocs had dominated parliament: the center-left and post-Solidarity electoral blocs. But in 2001 and 2005, both of these groupings imploded, to be replaced by a duopoly of Law and Justice, in office from 2005 to 2007,[4] and Civic Platform, in power from 2007 to 2015.

This divide between the two blocs was increasingly cultural, subsuming a number of other cleavages. As early as the 2005 and 2007 elections, as Jasiewicz (2008, 8–9) summarizes it, "the PO emphasized its commitment to individual liberties, procedural democracy, and entrepreneurial freedom as the basis of economic growth," finding support in the major urban areas in the northwest of the country. The PiS, on the contrary, advanced ideas of social solidarity and later ran on a combination of appeals to traditional values and populist economic policies, appealing to voters in small and medium-sized towns, generally in the southeast. But the PiS also sought to tap into economic

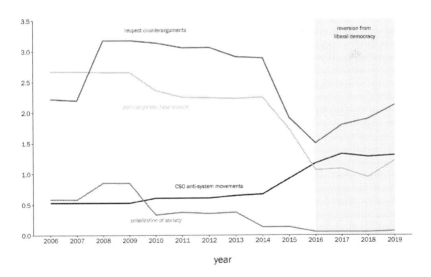

Figure 3: Polarization in Poland, 2006–2019.

---

[4] The PiS-led governing coalition included two parties that were even more overtly populist in their orientation than the PiS: Self-Defense of the Republic of Poland (Samoobrona Rzeczypospolitej Polskiej, or just Self-Defense) and the League of Polish Families (Liga Polskich Rodzin, or LPR).

nationalism, Euroskepticism, and resentment at the political and business elites of
the so-called Third Republic, an elite that was seen as corrupt, criminal and even
a "post-Communist residua."

The long absence from power from 2007 to 2015 allowed the PiS to nurture
these ideas, some of which took on conspiratorial colors. In particular, the plane
crash of 2010 in Smolensk, which decimated the Polish political elite of both
parties and killed Lech Kaczyński, drew his brother Jaroslaw in a darker, more
conspiratorial direction as he used the tragedy to galvanize his followers.

The PiS cause was aided, however, by the complacency of incumbents,
a political scandal in 2014 (the "tape affair") that – as in Brazil – revealed
government ministers as out of touch with the electorate and the onset of the
migration crisis. A June 2015 survey found that 72 percent of respondents were
dissatisfied not only with the incumbents but with Poland's political system. It
was precisely this broader disaffection with the Polish political elite that PiS
mobilized in both the presidential election of 2015 – in which the PiS scored
a major upset – and the parliamentary elections later in the year. Not only did the
left fail to win any seats in parliament, but two new parties to the right of PiS –
Kukiz'15 and Renewal of the Republic Freedom and Hope [KORWIN] –
captured over 13 percent of the popular vote.

It is important to underscore that the PiS vote share, at 37.6 percent of the
popular vote, was by no means overwhelming. Moreover, a number of analyses
of the election have demonstrated how the waste of left votes was crucial to
subsequent PiS dominance; we take up that issue in Section 3. Nonetheless, the
case shows that polarization cannot necessarily be understood by reference to
socioeconomic forces alone; rather, politicians play a key role in stoking
underlying social divisions, capitalizing on them for electoral gain.

2.5 The United States, 2016–2019

Given the idiosyncratic nature of the Trump campaign and presidency, it might be
thought that polarization in the United States is a relatively recent development.
As Figure 4 shows, however, all of the polarization indicators we use for
comparative purposes except "respect counterarguments" had begun to shift
over the course of the 2000s. Moreover, standard narratives on the sources of
elite polarization find its origins in the gradual breakup of the New Deal coalition
from the mid-1960s (Mikey, Levitsky & Way 2017; Abramowitz and Webster
2016) or even earlier (Shickler 2016). Race played a crucial role in this process.
The Democratic party splintered with the rise of the civil rights movement, the
passage of the Civil Rights and Voting Rights Acts of 1964–1965, and the
defection of the so-called Dixiecrats. Southern Republicans started to gain vote

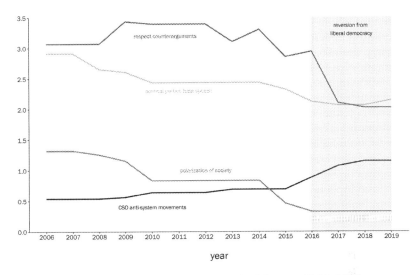

Figure 4: Polarization in the United States, 2006–2019.

share, first in presidential elections then in House and Senate contests, and ultimately became the dominant party in state legislatures as well. The great sorting of American political parties into more homogenous blocs had begun.

This "conflict extension" – the loading of more and more differences onto the left/right one – included a host of sensitive wedge issues related to other fundamental changes in American society over the course of the 1970s and 1980s: the decline of the traditional family, the entry of women into the workforce, and the rise of the women's and gay rights movements. Many of the related policy issues, such as abortion, subsequently divided the country on religious and moral beliefs as well as race. But these divisions increasingly coincided with party affiliation, especially among white voters (for example, Mann & Orenstein 2012; Mickey, Levitsky & Way 2017). As the New Deal coalition imploded, the Republican party began its well-documented shift to the right, first signaled in the Goldwater candidacy but carried forward by a succession of insurgents such as Pat Buchannan, Phyllis Shlafly, Newt Gingrich and ultimately Donald Trump.

The increasing diversity of the American electorate extended attitudes with respect to race to immigrants. The share of the foreign born in the United States bottomed out at about 5 percent in 1970 but rose to near 15 percent by 2016, a tripling of the immigrant share. Abrajano and Hajnal (2017) find that attitudes toward immigration – probably the dominant issue in the 2016 election campaign – were powerful predictors of voters' stances on a wide array of other issues. There is now ample evidence that racial resentment, ethnonationalism and racial prejudice played a decisive role in explaining vote choice in both the

2012 and 2016 elections (Abramowitz 2016; Knuckey & Kim 2016; Tesler 2016; Morgan & Lee 2017).

Finally, divisions over race and culture comingled in complex ways with economic grievances rooted in globalization, technological change, and ultimately stagnant wage growth and rising inequality. McCarty, Poole and Rosenthal (2016) were the first to note the near-lockstep correlation between the increase in inequality, which accelerated in the 1980s, and measures of Congressional polarization. The Global Financial Crisis only increased these divisions. Wide swaths of the population were left out of the modest recovery of the Obama years. Studies have noted how the Trump vote – resting on distinctive populist appeals – was associated with economic factors at the district level such as exposure to trade (Autor et al. 2017), the distinctive problems facing smaller metropolitan areas (Florida 2016), and social markers such as poor health, lower social mobility and weak social capital (Rothwell 2017).

While there is consensus that the United States is more divided, there is significant debate on whether polarization is an elite or mass phenomenon (see McCarty 2019 for an overview). In a succession of studies, Morris Fiorina (2008, 2017) has argued that divisions between the parties can be traced to elites and activists and that polarization in the public has not fundamentally increased over the last forty years. Rather, parties are more tightly "sorted or more homogenously ideological as liberals gravitated to the Democrats and conservatives to the Republicans." This view has been vigorously – and in our view successfully – challenged by those tracking the increasing polarization of the mass public (most notably Abramowitz and Webster 2016).

But for our purposes, the distinction between sorting and polarization is moot if the divisions between the parties are in fact cast in increasingly "us/them" or even affective or tribal terms. Moreover, some of the predicted effects of such polarization noted already are clearly visible in the United States. Polarization has resulted in an inability to compromise around common policy objectives. The Republican strategy toward Obama – masterminded by Senate majority leader Mitch McConnell – exemplified these effects. McConnell openly stated his party's objective was to block any initiative that Obama might propose. The number of those expressing a "great deal" or "quite a lot" of confidence in Congress had seen a secular decline over decades, but it bottomed out in single digits in 2014–2016, and some studies even noted a shocking decline in support for democracy itself (Mounk 2018).

There can be little question that Trump knew how to both capitalize on – and stoke – the manifold social divisions and disaffection with government that boiled over during the Obama years. But activists in civil society played a role in pulling the Republican party further to the right as well. One manifestation of this process was the mobilization of white, conservative and evangelical voters in the Tea Party movement, which came to focus increasingly on two of Obama's signature policy innovations: the fiscal policy necessary to counter the recession and health care. The early Tea Party movement drew sharp "us/them" distinctions around welfare targeting immigrants, minorities, and youth, and those programs like Social Security and Medicare that were directed towards the deserving, and not coincidentally older citizens (Skocpol & Williamson 2016). Trump's understanding of these issues accounts for his lack of interest in mainstream conservative issues such as entitlement reform and, along with his stance on trade, was responsible for giving his campaign its populist flavor.

The appeal of anti system political forces — another one of the effects of polarization that we highlight – was visible in a variety of other fringe right-wing movements that surfaced or expanded during the Obama years, from citizen militias to a plethora of hate groups (Neiwert 2017). Studiously using "dog whistle" politics that drew on these extremist tropes, Trump used three main appeals in the Republican primaries: his attacks on Mexican immigrants and Muslims; a protectionist trade policy and wider assault on multilateralism; and a deeper, more encompassing narrative about the corruption of Washington and the coastal elites. These various ideas came together in his nostalgic promise to "make America great again."

Perhaps the most compelling evidence for the role that polarization played in the 2016 elections is the rise of what Iyengar and Westwood (2015) have identified as affective polarization and negative partisanship. The 2016 election pitted two relatively unpopular candidates against one another. Not only was crossing party lines unthinkable, but, in line with the Svolik (2018) model referenced earlier, supporters of Donald Trump acquiesced to, and even embraced, promises that were clearly of dubious legality. These included surveilling and closing mosques, targeting the families of terrorists, cutting funding to sanctuary cities, and opening an investigation into Hillary Clinton and even jailing her. It proved a short step from promising these derogations to actually pursuing them.

2.6 Conclusion: Coming to Power

Political polarization is a circumstance that potential autocrats exploit. As the cases of Brazil and the United States both show, polarization raises risks for democracy because of its effects on the functioning of government and public disaffection. In all three cases, polarization was associated with increased support for extremist candidates and parties, placing a centripetal pull on established parties as well. Polarization also weakens support for the checks on government that are integral to liberal democracy. In all three cases we considered, candidates signaled their willingness to push against the constraints on executive discretion, an approach to democratic politics that we call "majoritarian."

Yet as we have seen from the cases of Poland and the United States, political division is also a circumstance that autocrats help create. The use of divisive messages to mobilize electoral support and demonize oppositions does not itself constitute backsliding if we define the concept as a form of purposeful institutional change. Once in office, however, it remains a political strategy that autocrats use to mobilize core supporters.

Given the weakening of centrist parties and the direct, popular appeal autocrats seem to enjoy, it might be thought that their power was rooted in surges of support and significant electoral majorities. In fact, this image of the autocrat is misleading. As the very concept of polarization suggests, both elites and electorates in polarized settings are sharply divided.

We do not find evidence that backsliding is only a creature of presidentialism. Nonetheless, the type of democracy – parliamentary versus presidential and the rules for presidential election – play an important role in precisely how autocrats come to office and the legislative support they subsequently enjoy. In five of our cases – Bolivia, Dominican Republic, Hungary, Russia and Venezuela – autocrats came to power with absolute majorities of the popular vote. Not coincidentally, all of these cases except Hungary were presidential. One other case can be considered an example of majority victories for an autocrat. In Brazil, Jair Bolsonaro fell just short of winning the presidency in the first round (46.0 percent) and won the second with 55.1 percent.

Yet it is worth noting that in Venezuela, Russia and Brazil newly elected presidents did not control their legislatures; indeed, newly formed party vehicles for Chávez and Putin controlled only a handful of seats (Movement for Socialism in Venezuela 14.8 percent and Unity in Russia, 16.2 percent). While Evo Morales enjoyed an absolute majority of the popular vote and seat shares in the lower house, his Movement for Socialism party did not have an outright majority in the Senate. Bolsonaro also confronted a highly fragmented legislature. The Social Liberty Party, which he briefly recruited as a personalist vehicle, secured only 11.7 percent of all votes cast for the Chamber of Deputies and 11.3 percent of popular votes cast in Senate elections.

In the remainder of cases, autocrats came to power with less than an outright majority of the popular vote. These cases, in turn, can be divided into two groups. Serbia, the United States and Zambia saw knife-edge elections;

polarization was reflected in extremely close contests. In Serbia, the SNS fell slightly short of a majority, with 48.4 percent of the popular vote, but this was a landslide for its parliamentary system; as we will see in Section 3 the SNS was able to form a coalition that controlled 63.2 percent of seats. Edgar Lungu also won a significant plurality of the popular vote in Zambia (48.3 to 46.7 for Hakainde Hichilema) but fell short of a majority because of minor party candidates. Until the elections of 2016 he also confronted a hostile legislature in which his Patriotic Front did not have a majority. In the United States, Donald Trump actually lost the popular vote to Hillary Clinton (46.1 percent to 48.2 percent), winning the presidency in the electoral college (304 votes to 227). Although Republicans maintained control of both the Senate and House, that control was narrow and the party lost the House in the mid term elections of 2018.

In the remainder of the cases, backsliding occurred under rulers or parties that came to power with a plurality of the popular vote but far short of 50 percent of the total vote share. Ecuador and Nicaragua were presidential, and neither Correa's nor Ortega's parties held majorities in the legislature (although Ortega's FSLN did enjoy a coalition agreement that provided him a majority). Greece, North Macedonia, Poland, Turkey and Ukraine are parliamentary. The elected governments in all of these countries faced robust oppositions, both in the legislature and from the wider public.

Given that autocrats did not typically come to power with overwhelming majorities, how did they manage to parley narrow electoral victories into purposeful institutional change? It is to this next step in the backsliding process – turning votes into seats and seats into legislative abdication – that we turn in Section 3.

3 Constitutions in the Balance: Parties, Legislatures and the Collapse of the Separation of Powers

As we argued in Section 2, autocrats mobilize support on the basis of polarizing narratives and a willingness to depart from the institutional, procedural and normative constraints of democratic rule. But backsliding itself is not simply about political appeals. Rather it is the outcome of efforts on the part of executives to restructure the constitutional order: to reduce horizontal checks on the executive; weaken the protection of political and civil liberties; and ultimately attack the integrity of the electoral system itself.

In this section, we start with the puzzle raised at the end of Section 2. The fragmentation or collapse of centrist parties, or their capture by extremists, typically sets the stage for backsliding. But as we have seen, autocrats do not necessarily come to office enjoying legislative or popular-vote majorities. We outline how presidents overcame opposition in their own parties, in separately elected legislatures, or – in the case of parliamentary systems – from coalition partners. We start with three Latin American cases – Venezuela, Bolivia and Ecuador – in which autocratic presidents formed constitutional assemblies that circumvented existing legislatures altogether. These cases are admittedly extreme, but precisely for that reason they demonstrate how legislative abdication plays in the backsliding process.

In our other cases, the capture of legislatures occurred through less dramatic means. We find two factors aided autocrats' electoral success. First, polarization and the attendant hollowing-out of the political center created coordination problems as existing parties factionalized or the party system itself fragmented. Autocrats exploited these circumstances, capitalizing on the failure of oppositions to coalesce around the political threat and forge new political coalitions. Second, we also find that disproportionality in the allocation of legislative seats allowed autocrats to lock in their legislative dominance and use it to expand executive prerogative.

Once installed as heads of government, autocrats gain access to significant organizational resources that can be used in these efforts. With control of the executive branch comes command of the bureaucracy, military and security apparatus as well as public media. Moreover, executives typically have some discretion – often quite significant – that they can use to bend the state apparatus to their will.

Ultimately, however, the success of illiberal projects depends not only on the capture of executive office by illiberal politicians but also on the support – or at least acquiescence – they muster from other branches of government. The most significant step in this regard comes when ruling parties enjoy majorities in the legislature, either outright or in coalition; this is particularly true when those parties are effectively controlled by the autocrat (Rhodes-Purdy & Madrid 2020). Control of the legislature has several important effects. First, it eliminates a pivotal source of oversight, widening the opportunities for political corruption and abuse of power and allowing executives to deploy prosecutors and law enforcement agencies against political opponents. Second, control of the legislature sets the stage for the weakening of horizontal checks, a process we call the collapse of the division of powers. Legislative control allows executives to stack the judiciary and independent executive agencies, including election monitoring bodies, with loyalists. Finally, through both constitutional reforms and ordinary legislation, legislatures can delegate additional formal powers to the executive, not only *expanding* the autocrat's powers – a process we take up in more detail in Section 4 – but *extending* it by eliminating term limits as well.

3.1 Frontal Assault: Creating New Constitutional Assemblies in Venezuela, Ecuador and Bolivia

In Venezuela, Ecuador and Bolivia newly elected populist presidents sought to restructure the political system through constitutional assemblies dominated by political loyalists (Stoyan 2020). The long-term erosion of support for established parties opened the door to the elimination of existing legislative veto points. In Venezuela, the election of Hugo Chávez in 1998 was preceded by the near collapse of two formerly dominant and deeply entrenched parties, the AD and Copei. Already by 1993, their combined share of the presidential vote had fallen to 46 percent from over 90 percent in preceding elections. In the contest that swept Chávez to power in 1998, they could muster only 11 percent of the popular vote between them.

We see a similar pattern in the other two countries. In Ecuador, support for the four traditional parties that competed for the presidency had declined from an average of 70 percent between 1984 and 1998 to under 30 percent in 2006. In Bolivia, conservative forces were able to regroup temporarily into a new party, PODEMOS, which offered more robust opposition than in the other two cases. Nevertheless, the vote shares of the three parties that had rotated in the presidency during the 1980s and 1990s (the MNR, MIR and ADN) had nearly disappeared by 2005, the year Evo Morales was elected.

Although populist presidents had the political advantage of broad popular support, however, opposition parties initially held on to enough congressional seats to check executive overreach. In Venezuela, the AD and Copei lost control of the Chamber of Deputies but retained twenty-seven of fifty-four Senate seats. In Ecuador, Rafael Correa's personal party vehicle, Alianza-PAIS, did not put forward candidates for Congress, ceding the ground to parties allied with Álvaro Noboa, his rival for the presidency in the 2006 election. Together with allies, Noboa's party (PRIAN) controlled close to two-thirds of the congressional seats. In Bolivia, the MAS captured 73 of the 130 seats in the lower house, but only 12 of the 27 Senate seats, finishing second to PODEMOS.

Chávez, with Correa and Morales following the Venezuelan template, each campaigned on promises to summon new constitutional assemblies that would "re-found" the democracies of their respective countries. All three capitalized on widespread disillusion with existing political institutions. But with institutional leverage in the legislature, opposing political forces initially had the authority to limit the powers of the new constitutional assemblies. Overcoming their rearguard resistance involved prolonged, sometimes violent, confrontations. But in all three cases new assemblies dominated by presidential loyalists were able to bypass existing legislatures in whole or part, effectively demonstrating how the removal of legislative checks has wide-ranging political consequences.

In Venezuela, Chávez launched his presidency by pressing the Supreme Court to authorize a referendum on constitutional reform. With the Court's reluctant acquiescence, the referendum posed two questions: whether to establish a constituent assembly; and what the voting rules should be for electing it. In the post-election honeymoon, both passed with overwhelming majorities (92.4 and 86.5 percent), albeit with very high abstention rates (63 percent). The referendum dramatically expanded the mandate that Chávez had received in the presidential election five months earlier. Most importantly, simple-majority voting rules permitted Chavistas to completely dominate the new assembly, with only six of the 125 members elected from the opposition.

A debate immediately broke out about whether the Assembly was ultimately the highest legislative body in the land. In August 1999, the members of the Assembly, supported by Chavista activists, physically occupied the parliament building, "deactivated" the Congress, where opposition parties still had leverage, and declared the Assembly the "originating" body authorized to legislate in the place of Congress. This view was effectively confirmed in a second referendum held in December in which 71.8 percent voted in favor of a constitution effectively drafted in closed committees. Again, the Supreme Court yielded to the political pressure to approve the results, and, as Corrales (2018, 122) points out, the only institutions left standing "were the presidency and the constituent assembly, where the president had a near monopoly."

Predictably, the new constitution that emerged from this process vastly increased the powers of the president and created a unicameral legislature more easily controlled by the ruling party. In August 2000, Chávez loyalists gained 60 percent of the seats in it. In 2005, his coalition captured 100 percent control of the seats when opposition parties boycotted the election. In 2006 he solidified his legislative power by reorganizing formerly separate Chavista factions into a new ruling party, the United Socialist Party of Venezuela (PSUV).

In the early 2000s, the new government was repeatedly challenged by general strikes, a prolonged work stoppage in the petroleum sector and even a short-lived coup d'etat before being helped by a sharp upswing in petroleum prices in 2003–2004. But opposition parties had also been fatally weakened by the creation of new institutions – the Constituent Assembly and unicameral legislature – and the rewriting of the constitution. The opposition's institutional leverage had vanished.

In Ecuador, Rafael Correa – influenced by the Venezuelan precedent – began to campaign for a new constitution in the second round of the 2006 presidential election. The proposal had strong support from indigenous, feminist and environmental movements, as well as wide backing within the general public at large. Correa captured 57 percent of the vote, after finishing second in the first round to banana king Álvaro Naboa (23 percent to 27 percent).

Once in office, Correa's call for a referendum to establish a constituent assembly quickly brought him into conflict with the opposition in Congress over how much authority the assembly would be granted. The ensuing struggle led to a virtual collapse of Ecuador's weak and discredited political institutions. Correa's opponents in Congress responded to the referendum initiative by moving to fire four members of the Electoral Council that had approved it. Correa in turn responded by pressing the Council to remove fifty-seven opposition legislators who had blocked a vote on the referendum and to suspend their right to run for the constitutional assembly. The Constitutional Court entered the fray by ruling against the dismissal, but a majority of the remaining members of Congress voted to remove all nine judges from the Court and to proceed with the referendum.

In April 2007, the referendum was approved by almost 87 percent of the popular vote. In the election for delegates to the Assembly, Correa's Alianza-PAIS party captured 80 of the 130 seats, with his social movement allies winning most of the rest. The traditional opposition parties were almost completely marginalized; Noboa's PRIAN party, which held the plurality of seats in the old Congress, gained only eight in the Assembly. Once seated, the Assembly voted overwhelmingly (110 to 18) to dismiss Congress on grounds of corruption. Congress was ultimately forced to accept the supremacy of the Assembly.

The new constitution was ratified in September 2008 by almost 64 percent of the vote, and Correa was the principle winner. Among other things, the president gained the right to dissolve the legislature, to control the Central Bank and to run for reelection (Corrales 2018, 184). The losers were the opposition parties and institutions of horizontal accountability. Subsequent elections for Congress in 2009 and 2013 consolidated Correa's control.

The rise of Evo Morales and the restructuring of the Bolivian constitution proved even more contentious than in Venezuela and Ecuador, resulting initially in a more limited changes in the constitutional order. In past years, proposals to convene a constituent assembly had come from across the political spectrum, and Congress eventually provided the two-thirds majority to pass Morales's initiative by regular law. But the opposition held adequate seats to force compromises on rules governing elections and procedures within the Assembly. Unlike in Venezuela and Ecuador, moreover, opposition political elites regrouped into a new party, PODEMOS. The party retained enough popular support in the mineral-rich eastern provinces to mobilize a powerful, sometimes violent opposition to Morales's power grab.

The pivotal conflict was over a provision imposed by the Senate that required a two-thirds majority for all Assembly decisions, giving the opposition an effective veto over proposals coming from the lower house that Morales dominated. Morales supporters engaged in a variety of attempts to abrogate or evade this restriction, including shifting the site of the assembly meeting, physically blocking the entry of opposition politicians, and attempting to ram through a constitution during an opposition boycott. These moves, however, triggered extensive opposition protests and violent confrontations with MAS supporters that subsided only after negotiations sponsored by the OAS, the UN, the EU, and the Union of South American Nations (UNASUR) generated a compromise.

Morales was forced to retreat temporarily on a number of key issues, including a commitment (later disavowed) not to run for reelection in 2014. But although Morales did not get the formal power that he wanted from the Assembly, he did get a major political boost for having engineered a new constitution which incorporated extensive social rights for his indigenous constituency (Stoyan 2020).

With the commodity boom of the mid-2000s, moreover, the political and institutional momentum shifted decisively in Morales's favor. In the 2009 general elections, the MAS gained control of both houses of Congress, allowing Morales to run for reelection in 2014 and engineer referenda that could have extended his tenure until 2030. The opposition Convergencia, a successor party to PODEMOS, was almost entirely marginalized, with MAS holding 88 of the 130 seats in the lower chamber and twenty-six of the thirty-six Senate seats. As in the other cases, the legislature had been converted into an extension of presidential power.

These three cases clearly stand apart in the unusual way that presidents gained control of legislatures through the creation of parallel institutions. In all three cases, initial steps that had some legal foundation quickly bled over into a collapse of the separation of power. Yet the cases demonstrate the central point of this section: that legislatures matter. In Bolivia, the constituent assembly did not directly lead to executive overreach, but in all three countries autocrats sought to use these bodies to bypass legislative constraints.

3.2 Letting Autocrats In: Party Fragmentation, Coordination and Disproportionality

In the other countries in our sample, control of legislatures happened in a less dramatic fashion. How did autocratic leaders and parties – typically associated with political extremes – construct legislative majorities that would do the executive's bidding? First, the hollowing-out of the political center implied by polarization can lead to coordination problems. Parties that share aversion to the autocrat do not necessarily coalesce to stop him. Second, however, we see a surprising role for disproportionality in autocratic ascent. In a number of cases, electoral rules turned popular vote pluralities into outright legislative majorities and even supermajorities.

3.3 The Coordination Problem

By definition, the polarization of the party system implies either moves to the extremes on the part of existing parties – with the number and identity of the major parties staying relatively fixed – or the emergence of new extreme parties, with centrist parties splintering, weakening or even disappearing altogether. Examples of the former phenomenon would include Donald Trump's capture of the Republican party during the 2016 primaries in the United States, the remaking of FIDESZ and PiS under the leadership of Viktor Orbán in Hungary, and Lech and Jarosław Kaczyński in Poland.

Where autocratic leaders gain control of a major party, they benefit from established political organizations and voter loyalties. But they also push those parties away from previous programmatic commitments, often in quite surprising and counterintuitive ways (Rhodes-Purdy & Madrid 2020). Donald Trump, for example, ran on a populist platform that included opposition not only to immigration but also to the free trade positions of the Republican party. He also quickly signaled his lack of interest in entitlement reforms that had long preoccupied fiscal conservatives. An open primary system allowed him to appeal to voters directly on the basis of these unorthodox policy positions, and he roundly trounced a field of more traditional Republican candidates.

A similar process is visible in Hungary, where Orbán initially entered politics as a liberal democrat. By the mid-1990s, Fidesz began to aggressively court more conservative voters with nationalist and populist appeals. Fidesz defeated the Socialist and liberal parties in 1998, but the latter regained office in 2002 and were reelected in 2006. Political support for the socialists fell drastically, however, following a devastating corruption scandal and sharp economic contraction during the global financial crisis. Orbán, as well as the far-right Jobbik party, mobilized mass demonstrations against the government in the fall of 2006 that further polarized the public. These moves set the stage for Orbán's dramatic electoral triumph in 2010 on a platform that combined economic populism with blistering attacks on the "corrupt elites" represented by parties on the left.

Polarization can also occur when party systems effectively implode, with incumbent centrist parties (and in our sample, particularly those on the center-left) losing ground to parties on the extremes. This was true in the three cases described in the previous section and in countries otherwise as diverse as Brazil, Greece and Turkey. In all of these cases, ruling coalitions or long-standing parties experienced a rapid deflation of support in the election that brought governments associated with bacisliding to power.

Brazil and Greece provide examples. The most salient feature of the 2018 election in Brazil was the severe weakening of the two parties that had dominated presidential election contests since the mid-1990s: the PT and the PSDB. Lula, the popular leader of the PT, had been jailed in the corruption scandal and was unable to run in 2018. His replacement – Fernando Haddad – polled less than 30 percent in the first round of presidential voting, only narrowly preventing Jair Bolsonoro – with over 46 percent – from winning an outright majority. The candidate of the PSDB, Geraldo Alckmin, received less than 5 percent of the vote. The sharp decline in support for the PSDB and the PT was also evident in the congressional elections. The PSDB representation in the Chamber of Deputies fell from fifty-four to twenty-nine seats between 2014 and 2018; the PT went from sixty-eight to fifty-five. The PMDB, a perennial swing party, saw its representation fall from sixty-six to thirty-four seats.

Although an ambiguous case, V-Dem data identifies Greece's backsliding beginning in 2017. The episode is identified with the government headed by Alexis Tsipras's Coalition of the Radical Left (Syriza), a left-wing populist party that came to power in the two elections of 2015 (January and September). As in Brazil, these elections marked the rapid unraveling of the Greek party system in the wake of the financial crisis of the early 2010s. From the end of the military dictatorship in 1974, power had alternated between governments led by either the center-left PASOK or the center-right New Democracy. In each of the elections of the 2000s (2000, 2004, 2007, 2009), one of these parties was able to secure at least 40 percent of the popular vote and gain an outright majority of legislative seats. In the election of 2012, New Democracy won only 18.9 percent of the popular vote (although translating that into over one-third of seats). New Democracy bounced back to nearly 30 percent of the popular vote in the elections of 2012, but Syriza broke through because of the continuing decline in the fortunes of PASOK and the left generally. In the wake of this collapse, extremist parties on both the left and right gained ground, including ANEL and the anti-immigrant Golden Dawn, the party symbol of which was disturbingly redolent of the Nazi swastika.

Where party systems polarize, a second dynamic comes into play: which leaders and parties are most effective in capitalizing on changing voter loyalties? It is no accident that backsliding is typically associated with the personal appeal of particular leaders: Putin, Chávez, Correa, Orbán, Trump, Erdoğan.

More recently, Rodrigo Duterte has shown similar political skills in the Philippines. These autocratic leaders prove highly effective in mobilizing support over the heads of established parties: through public appearances, mass rallies, savvy use of social media and above all through polarizing populist appeals (Kenny 2017).

In some cases, autocrats and their parties forge opportunistic coalitions precisely around the personal charisma, electoral clout and ultimately executive power of the autocrat (Rhodes-Purdy & Madrid 2020). Party building is a result – not a cause – of autocratic success as weaker political actors bandwagon to strength. For example, Vladimir Putin's United Russia emerged out of the confusing stew of parties represented in the Second State Duma (1995–1999). United Russia's predecessor, the Unity bloc, was formed just before the 1999 Duma elections. In the same year, Putin was appointed interim prime minister, and his popularity soared in the wake of forceful military intervention in Chechnya. Unity's support also rose, and the party ended up securing the second-largest share of both votes and seats – behind the Communist Party – in the 1999 elections. This result signaled strongly that Putin would probably be elected to the presidency in 2000. His main opponents dropped out of the presidential race, and Unity merged with its biggest competitor in 2001, also absorbing a number of independents. By the elections for the fourth Duma in 2003, the party held not only an absolute majority of seats but 69 percent of them; subsequent reforms of the Duma further consolidated Putin's grip on the legislature (Remington 2008).

Turkey demonstrates a similar dynamic, with Erdoğan's AKP gaining strength over time. As in Venezuela, Greece and Brazil, the pivotal election (in 2002) occurred against a fraught backdrop of a financial collapse. In addition to the crisis, high electoral thresholds favored the AKP, and the party system underwent a marked consolidation: outside of the AKP, only the center-left CHP (Republican People's Party) managed to win any parliamentary seats at all. Erdoğan campaigned and governed initially from the center-right, albeit with subtle Islamist appeals. Once in office, however, majoritarian and Islamist tones became stronger (Keyman & Gumuscu 2014, 45–54). Erdoğan represented himself as the standard-bearer of the "virtuous people" against an array of enemies – nonreligious Kurds, Alevis, liberals, leftists and seculars (Yabanci 2016, 598) – and his dominance of the legislature ultimately set the stage for a weakening of checks on his executive powers.

The flip side of autocratic success is the failure of incumbents to counter extremist challengers. We see this process in the collapse of long-prominent socialist parties in Eastern Europe, including in Serbia, Hungary and Poland (Grzymala-Bussen 2019). Poland provides a particularly striking example

(Fomina & Kucharczyk 2016). As in all of the transition cases in Eastern Europe, Polish society was divided by tensions related to the legacy of the Communist past and widening inequalities associated with marketization. But the Polish economy had continued to grow under the incumbent Civic Platform (PO) government, and the country had even largely escaped the ravages of the global financial crisis. It is hard to argue that the results of the pivotal 2015 election reflected a strong rejection of the status quo. In fact, the PO's share of the vote, together with that of its allies, was actually higher than that of the PiS (40.4 to 37.6 percent). The outcome reflected the strategies of the competing parties and the unintended consequences of the electoral system. The incumbent Civic Platform (CO) encountered competition from the newly formed liberal party (MODERN), which split the centrist bloc and led to a high percentage of wasted votes. For the first time in its post-communist history, a single party enjoyed an outright majority in the Sejm, but it was one that had pushed the Polish political system toward its extremes.

The rise of Daniel Ortega provides a similar illustration of coordination failures, this time in a presidential system and with the right rather than the left on the losing end. Ortega initially achieved the presidency in 2006 through the exploitation of divisions within the then-incumbent Liberal party. The source of these splits was a massive corruption scandal that engulfed former Liberal president Arnoldo Alemán starting in 1999. To protect himself and his allies, Alemán forged a *Pacto* with Ortega that allowed them jointly to share appointments to the judiciary, the electoral council and other centers of power. Ortega had polled only about 35 percent in previous presidential elections, but the agreement lowered the threshold for winning the 2006 presidential election from 40 to 35 percent with a required five-point margin over the first runner-up. He won his first presidential election over divided Liberal competitors with 38 percent of the vote.

In the aftermath, Ortega leveraged his initial victory into dominance over the political system as a whole: not surprisingly, many of his early political initiatives dealt precisely with the electoral system. In 2009, Sandinista loyalists on the Supreme Court overturned a ban on consecutive presidential terms, allowing Ortega to run for reelection in 2011. Exploiting oil subsidies from Venezuela, the government expanded social benefits, and popular support for the fractious Liberals withered. In the 2011 elections, Ortega's vote share rose to 62.5 percent from 37 percent in 2006, and Sandistas won sixty-three of the ninety-two seats in the National Assembly with a 60 percent popular vote share; liberal factions competed over the remainder.

3.4 Electoral Rules and Disproportionality

As a number of the cases discussed have already suggested, disproportionality – differences between popular vote and legislative seats shares – also played an important role in the rise of autocrats.[5] Table 5 provides a simple – indeed crude – measure of disproportionality by comparing the popular vote share for the backsliding party with the seats it gained in the lower house. It starts with the "founding" elections that brought autocrats to power but provides information on subsequent elections as well; we omit the cases of Venezuela, Ecuador and Bolivia discussed already due to the fundamental institutional discontinuities associated with the formation of constituent assemblies and Brazil because of its particularly fragmented party system.

In seven of the twelve remaining cases – the Dominican Republic, Hungary, Poland, Russia, Turkey, the United States and Zambia – the party associated with the backsliding leader converted plurality vote shares into lower house majorities. But if we look at all subsequent elections, the list would expand to include Hungary and Serbia as well, representing nine of the twelve relevant cases.

In five of these, the wedge between the vote and seat share was large, exceeding 10 percentage points in at least one election. As we saw in Turkey, a 10 percent threshold for representation vastly magnified the AKP's seat share in the 2002 elections, allowing the party to translate 34 percent of the popular vote into 66 percent of legislative seats. All of the parties that had comprised the previous government failed to clear the threshold and were shut out of parliament entirely. The party's seat share fell in subsequent elections, but the AKP retained strong parliamentary majorities until 2015, enabling a succesion of legal and institutional changes that we take up in Section 4.

Finally, it is worth taking note of the Hungarian case, where disproportionality permitted not only large majorities but an outright constitutional supermajority. A 5 percent electoral threshold translated a 53 percent majority popular vote share into a 68 percent legislative supermajority. The seat share of the ousted Socialists fell from 43 percent in 2006 to 19 percent, and the center-right MDF and center-left Free Democrats failed to enter parliament at all. Vladimir Putin also enjoyed legislative supermajorities in the Dumas elected in 2007 and 2016, permitting him to push through fundamental constitutional changes.

Disproportionality clearly exists in consolidated democracies and is by no means a necessary nor a sufficient condition for backsliding to occur.

---

[5] It is beyond our scope here to detail the possible sources of disproportionality, let alone the large literature on measurement. But they include not only district magnitude and electoral thresholds but other restraints autocrats may place on oppositions.

Table 5: Lower House Vote and Seat Shares in Backsliding Cases

	Lower House Vote share/seat share (%)
Dominican Republic 2014-2018 PLD	2017: 41.8/55.0
Greece 2017-2019	
Syriza	2015 (September): 35.5/48.3
New Democracy	2019: 39.9/52.7
Hungary 2010-2019	2010: 53.5/68.1
FIDESZ	2014: 44.5/66.8
	2018: 47.5/66.8
North Macedonia 2010-2016	2008: 61.6/67.5
VMRO-DPMNE/Union for Integration	2011: 49.2/57.7
	2014: 44.5/49.6
	2018: 38.1/42.5
Nicaragua 2005-2019	2006: 37.6/41.3
FSLN	2011: 60.9/68.4
	2016: 65.9/70.0
Poland 2015-2019	2015: 37.6/51.1
Law and Justice: PiS	2019: 43.6/51.1
Russia 2000-2019	2003: 37.5/50.0
United Russia Party	2007: 64.3/70.0
	2011: 50.2/53.5
	2016: 55.2/76.2
Serbia 2013-2019	2014: 50.0/63.2
2014, SNS; 2016 Aleksandar Vučić-Serbia Wins coalition	2016: 48.3/63.2
Turkey 2010-2019	2002: 34.3/66.0
AKP (2018, People's Alliance, AKP and MHP)	2007: 46.7/66.0
	2011: 49.9/59.3
	2015: 40.9/46.9
	2018: 51.5/57.3
Ukraine 2010-2018	2012: 30.0/41.1
Party of the Regions from 2010; Petro Poroshenko Bloc 2014	2014: 21.8/31.2
United States 2016-2019	2016: 49.1/56.8
Republican Party	
Zambia Patriotic Front 2016-2019	2016: 42.0/51.3

Note: The first election shown is the one which first brought the illiberal party to power. Brazil is omitted because of its highly fragmented party system. Hungary, vote shares are for constituent (vs. list) seats. Ukraine: backsliding persisted despite a change in government with the 2014 presidential elections. For a list of all acronyms, see the online Appendix.

Nonetheless, we see a number of cases in which the leaders and parties associated with the backsliding episode only enjoyed pluralities, even if substantial by their countries' standards: Greece, North Macedonia, Nicaragua, Turkey (briefly in the mid-2010s) and Ukraine. Some of these coalitions proved extraordinarily fragile, but others proved viable by engaging parties similarly distant from the political center: in Greece, for example, the second Tsipras cabinet (September) was formed with a right-populist party – the Independent Greeks – that shared a number of Syriza's preoccupations. Yet backsliding leaders and parties frequently exploited dispoportionality to dominate legislatures; we now turn to the implications of these developments.

3.5 Compliant Legislatures: Collapsing the Division of Powers

Compliant legislatures have proved critical for legitimating and consolidating autocratic rule. In the more robust liberal democracies – most notably, the United States and Brazil – legislative opposition parties continued to provide important brakes on the centralization of executive power. Moreover, we can find numerous instances of executive abuses that are not rooted directly in legislative support. But in the large majority of backsliding cases, executive control over an autocratic party and legislative majorities allowed executives to expand their power at the expense of the judiciary and the legislature itself. In this section, we examine three ways that legislative acquiescence has been pivotal in this collapse of the separation of powers: by defaulting on oversight functions; by confirming appointments to the judiciary and executive and administrative agencies; and by ratifying "reforms" that expand executive authority outright.

3.5.1 Defaulting on Oversight

In important respects, what legislatures do *not* do is as important as the positive steps they undertake. Defaulting on oversight constitutes a major step in collapsing the mechanisms of horizontal accountability so essential to liberal democracy. The V-Dem legislative oversight index combines assessments of whether the legislature can routinely question and investigate executive branch officials, as well as the extent to which the executive is subject to oversight from opposition parties and from executive agencies such as the comptroller general or ombudsman. (Precise wording of these questions and data on the backsliding cases are provided in the online Appendix.)

Fifteen of the sixteen cases registered declines in legislative oversight during the backsliding episodes, with eleven falling significantly below the relevant regional benchmarks. Legislative oversight in the United States,

Brazil, Poland and Bolivia also fell below regional benchmarks, but confidence intervals overlapped. However, this might underestimate the importance of decline in these cases. Legislatures in the United States and Brazil began to decline from legistlative oversight scores that were initially far above that of their regional peers. Poland's ruling party – PiS – had a much narrower majority (just over 51 percent), which might account for the more limited character of its decline. In Bolivia, we have already seen how opportunities for oversight were severely limited by the fact that Evo Morales's MAS controlled over two-thirds of the legislative seats after the general election of 2009. Despite these partial exceptions, it is noteworthy that, out of sixteen backsliding cases, only Greece showed no change in the capacity of the legislature to exercise oversight (and it is probably the most ambiguous of the backsliding cases we consider).

The weakness or absence of legislative oversight can have pervasive consequences for the rest of the political system. Lack of oversight significantly reduces constraints on the executive with respect to the misuse of the bureaucracy and enables the use of public resources to target political enemies, harass and intimidate civil society groups, or engage in self-enrichment.

One particularly visible consequence of lack of legislative oversight is corruption. Freed from effective oversight, autocratic executives have deployed government contracts, regulatory authority and tax laws to forge alliances with crony capitalists while punishing private sector opponents. Bálint Magyar (2016), for example, has labeled Hungary a "post-communist mafia state" in this regard, documenting the way Viktor Orbán has deployed blackmail and threats of prosecution to force the sale of private firms to political allies and to divert funds to buy support from lower-level government and party officials. Crony capitalism has also been documented as an essential feature of backsliding in cases as diverse as Venezuela, Turkey, Serbia, Ukraine, Russia and the United States.

3.5.2 Stacking the Deck: Political Appointments

Captured legislatures, of course, did much more than look away: they took positive actions that weakened or dismantled other institutions of accountability. Crucial in this regard was support for executive appointments. Although executive discretion with regard to appointments varies across the cases, legislative approval of choices for high-level positions in the bureaucracy, independent agencies, law enforcement and the judiciary contributed to the expansion of autocratic power. In some cases, appointments were enabled by complementary administrative restructuring that created new layers of authority, altered rules of employment, or expanded the number of positions that autocrats and their legislative allies could fill.

The reorganization of judiciaries, law enforcement and independent electoral authorities has been particularly noteworthy in this regard. Once rulers had extended control over these crucial nodes of power, they could count on them to rule in ways that favored executive interests when challenged by political opponents. V-Dem data shown in Section 4 show substantial declines in the independence of the judiciary and electoral institutions in virtually all of the backsliding cases, declines that can typically be traced in part to legislative backing of executive appointments and organizational changes that expanded the executive's appointment powers.

In the United States, legislative approval of political loyalists has served to enlarge the power of the president and weakened crucial checks in the Department of Justice. Trump did face occasional Senate pushback on some of his choices for high-level cabinet and administrative positions. But in the context of charges of executive malfeasance, including impeachment over charges of election interference, Attorney General William Barr appeared to take crucial actions that helped to shield the president from closer legislative and public scrutiny.

Senate ratification of judicial appointments has also provided the president with crucial advantages. Political calculations, to be sure, have long been important components of presidential choices, and these had become increasingly contentious prior to the Trump presidency. In Obama's first term, Republicans resorted to the filibuster to block judicial appointments to an unprecedented degree; Democrats responded by shifting the rules on judicial votes from a 60 percent supermajority to simple majority. Republicans responded with the so-called nuclear option with respect to Supreme Court appointments, reducing the political pressure to nominate judicial moderates. Moreover, Trump appeared more openly partisan in his approach. He promised to appoint judges from nominees suggested by the Federalist Society, and he put them forward while openly denigrating the independence of the judiciary and challenging the impartiality of judges who disagreed with him.

Given the robust constitutional traditions of the American political system, and partisan turnover in executive appointments, Senate complicity in Trump's appointments has by no means obliterated the judicial and bureaucratic checks on presidential power. But even without the institutional reorganization or outright purges visible in other backsliding cases, such appointments worked to politicize the judiciary and formerly independent agencies.

In less-institutionalized democracies, legislative collaboration in the politicization of the judicial system and other nominally independent agencies has had even more far-reaching effects. In Venezuela, congressional majorities approved Chávez's initiative to appoint twelve loyalists to new positions on the Supreme Court in 2006, essentially destroying its independence. In Hungary, a constitutional reform approved by Orbán's supermajority in parliament enabled new judicial appointments by expanding the size of the Supreme Court. In 2013, the parliament approved further limitations on the Court's authority by allowing political appointees in the National Judicial Office to determine judicial appointments and even overrule previous constitutional judgments; we provide more examples of the collapse of the separation of powers in Section 4.

3.5.3 Expanding – and Extending – Executive Powers

Ratification of appointments and administrative reorganizations are not the only ways compliant legislatures enable executives to overreach into the authority of other branches. Since the infamous example of the Reichstag's Enabling Act of 1933, legislatures have ceded powers to the executive and – ipso facto – reduced their own. In the backsliding cases that we document here, this rarely takes the coup-like form of granting presidents or prime ministers emergency powers outright. Only in one case in our sample – Zambia in 2017 – did the autocrat's party rubber-stamp a state of emergency.[6] However, as the Latin American "frontal assault" cases show, backsliding is typically associated with the ceding of discretionary powers to the executive, allow them to lock in their policy preferences. Nor is such ceding of powers limited to the passing of regular laws. In twelve of the sixteen backsliding cases, backsliding was accompanied by constitutional revision or constitutional amendments, in some cases multiple ones.[7]

It is worth noting, finally, a particular way in which a number of legislatures facilitated fundamental constitutional reforms that expanded executive powers: by endorsing referenda. Referenda expose backsliding governments to the risk of embarrassing defeats, as occurred in 2016 when voters rejected a proposal to allow Bolivia's Evo Morales to run for a fourth term. But referenda have the advantage of permitting charismatic executives to make direct majoritarian appeals outside of normal electoral or legislative channels. Once referenda are authorized by the legislature or electoral authorities, governments can shape

---

[6] When Nicolás Maduro declared a state of emergency in Venezuela in 2016, it was precisely in the wake of a reversal of his electoral fortunes as the opposition had won a resounding electoral victory.

[7] The exceptions are Greece, Poland, Serbia and the United States, although in both Poland and Serbia similarly fundamental aims were achieved with extraordinary or regular legislation.

media coverage and use public resources to tilt the odds of success in the government's favor.

The variety of ways legislatures cede power to executives – whether through constitutional revision or amendment or normal law – and the precise powers that are ceded are explored in more detail in Section 4 and particularly in the case studies in the online Appendix. But it is important to emphasize the pervasiveness of efforts not only to *expand* executive powers but to *extend* them as well. Governments in seven of the sixteen cases in our sample undertook constitutional revisions or legislative initiatives or effectively forced judicial rulings that lifted prior term limits on executive office: Bolivia, the Dominican Republic, Ecuador, Nicaragua, Russia, Turkey and Venezuela. Interestingly, these seven cases represent all of the presidential systems in the sample except for the liberal democracies of the United States and Brazil. Efforts to evade term limits have become focal points for oppositions, most recently in Nicaragua and Bolivia, where Evo Morales was ultimately forced to step down. However, more autocratic regimes have been associated with long reigns on the part of their respective autocrats: fourteen years on the part of Hugo Chávez and, as of this writing, seventeen years on the part of Recep Tayyip Erdoğan and twenty years on the part of Vladimir Putin.

3.6 Conclusion

We started this section with a puzzle posed at the end of Section 2. How did elected autocrats gain control over legislatures, and with what effect? Our intuition is that the danger to democracy is enhanced considerably when autocrats exert strong authority over ruling parties and enjoy legislative support.

We began with an unusual set of extreme cases. The Venezuelan model, which spread in somewhat different form to Bolivia and Ecuador, rested on the creation of parallel constituent assemblies that dramatically expanded the powers of the respective presidents and weakened or abolished existing legislatures. Elsewhere, the route to legislative majorities was more circuitous and involved exploiting polarization and the splintering or capture of established parties. However we also found that disproportionality played a surprising role in locking in autocratic advantage.

We then reviewed how acquiescent legislative majorities allowed the executive to act without fear of oversight. Legislative control also freed the hand of the executive over appointments and thus control over the judiciary and other executive agencies, including the instruments of law enforcement and bodies tasked with staging and monitoring elections. As we will show in Section 4, the weaponization of the judiciary and executive is a major step toward the devolution into a competitive authoritarian regime. Legislative majorities under the control of executives also authorized the formal expansion of executive authority. They did this through outright constitutional revision, through regular legislation and through referenda that sidestep the usual checks on large-scale institutional change.

In sum, legislative majorities provided the legal foundation for attacks on other agencies of accountability; ironically, these majorities can result in a collapse of the very separation of executive and legislative powers that they are designed to embody. Even illiberal executives face an array of constraints from the judiciary, the press, civil society and other independent centers of power. In the backsliding cases, executives rarely – if ever – have the power to neutralize these centers in a single blow. But legislative majorities allowed them to chip away at these constraints incrementally. How this subsequent process unfolds is the subject of Section 4.

4 The Backsliding Process

As we showed in previous sections, backsliding is set in train by polarization, the rise of illiberal candidates and legislative acquiescence in the collapse in the separation of powers. In this section, we examine in more detail how autocrats – with somewhat varying powers – undermine the three defining components of liberal democracy: horizontal checks on executive discretion; political rights and civil liberties; and in some cases the integrity of the electoral system itself.

Horizontal checks on executives are designed to assure the rule of law: that executives and their agents comply with democratic and administrative procedure and abide by statute. In addition to the roles played by the legislature and judiciary, which we discussed in Section 3, these checks include administrative entities that are delegated powers and shielded – at least to some extent – from political manipulation. Yet a variety of other agencies impose crucial horizontal checks on executives, including those responsible for the census, for checking corruption and for guaranteeing the integrity of administrative processes. The scope of these bodies is arguably wider still, ranging from central banks to administrative agencies tasked with providing unbiased information: from budget offices to agencies responsible for regulating health and safety, financial markets, and the environment.

The second component of democracy at risk is the body of political rights and civil liberties that are central to democratic rule, particularly freedom of speech, assembly, association and – perhaps most fundamentally – physical integrity. These rights and liberties are significant to all individuals but

particularly to vulnerable minorities who often bear the brunt of early derogations from democratic rule. These rights and liberties also protect civil society
organizations, private enterprises and ultimately political parties as well.
Particularly important in this regard is the media, which acts as a check on
abuses of power and has a wider effect on the information environment, an issue
to which we return in Section 5.

Finally, autocrats undermine democracy by manipulating election-monitoring
institutions, tilting the electoral playing field decisively against oppositions and
engaging in outright fraud. A neutral electoral authority assures competitors free
ballot access for voters and an honest vote count. Meddling with the electoral
system constitutes a derogation of particular importance, as it goes to the
minimum requisite for a political system to be considered democratic at all.

Three priors inform our analysis of autocratic attacks on these interrelated
components of democratic rule. The first rests on an empirical regularity and is
definitional: backsliding is an incremental process that begins within
a democratic framework. Horizontal checks, rights and elections are not
abruptly dismantled through coups or the assertion of emergency powers.
Rather, they are undermined both through piecemeal legal changes and outright
violation of laws and norms.

Second, however, there are theoretical reasons why incremental changes
might favor the autocrat – why incrementalism itself has causal effect. The
components of liberal democracy are mutually constitutive. The integrity of
elections depends on horizontal checks and robust protection of rights. Rights,
in turn, depend on independent judiciaries, the rule of law and the accountability
provided by elections. Attacks on one of these institutional pillars of democracy
augments executive power, reduces constraints and thus creates the opportunity
for further derogations.

Finally, we hypothesize that the incremental nature of the backsliding process
has adverse effects through behavioral or social psychological mechanisms as
well. Individuals anchor expectations in the status quo. Marginal derogations from
both the law and established norms – "salami tactics," or what Przeworski (2019)
calls "stealth" – can normalize abuses and disorient oppositions and encourage
acquiescence. Autocrats are masters of ambiguity and obfuscation if not outright
disinformation, sowing confusion about the nature of the steps they are taking and
thus delaying effective responses. Oppositions may be acutely aware of these
derogations, but mass publics may not recognize that the playing field has tilted
until it is too late. The barrage of constitutionally dubious initiatives in the early
Orbán and Trump administrations provide a vivid example of this process.

The first section provides an overview of the backsliding process in our
sixteen cases. The second section elaborates some propositions about the

incremental nature of the backsliding process and illustrates with brief discussions of four cases that became models of the process and were even emulated elsewhere: Venezuela, Russia, Hungary and the United States. The third section discusses the conditions under which backsliding remains within a range of political practice that can be considered democratic and those under which democracies slide into authoritarian rule.

4.1 Backsliding: An Overview

Table 6 shows how the countries in our sample fared with respect to the three constitutive components of democracy that have structured our analysis. As a proxy for horizontal accountability, the first column provides point estimates for V-Dem's measure of high court independence. The second column focuses on the decline in civil liberties, using V-Dem estimates for repression of civil society organizations. The third column captures government effort – both directly and indirectly – to censor the media. Control over the media is a crucial component of the backsliding process as it shapes the information environment. The fourth column presents data on the integrity of the electoral system. As detailed in Table 6, each variable is scaled on a range from gross violations of democratic norms to strong compliance with them. We show these estimates at two points in time: the year immediately prior to the onset of backsliding and the year of the lowest score during the backsliding episode.

Since we have defined backsliding as departures from liberal democratic rule, the decline in scores shown in Table 6 should not surprise. Even so, the fact that the decline is generally spread across all of the institutional pillars of democratic rule provides indirect support for the intuition that the components of democracy are in fact mutually constituitive. Three cases in the sample – Greece, the United States and Ecuador – have at least one indicator that declined by less than .2 points on the 5-point scale. Yet in all three of those cases, other dimensions showed more significant deterioration.[8] In the other thirteen cases, we see declines in scores for all measures outlined.

Comparisons between scores immediately preceding the backsliding episodes and their nadirs also provide an indication of the incremental nature of the backsliding process. The time span between onset and low point is necessarily short for episodes that begin in 2016 or 2017 (Brazil, Greece, Poland and the United States). But in early backsliders such as Bolivia, Ecuador, Hungary, Nicaragua, Russia, Turkey and Venezuela, backsliding continued for a decade

---

[8] In the United States, high court independence actually improves, and CSO repression shows only small movement. Ecuador shows only small movement on the integrity of electoral institutions. Greece is the closest to an anomaly, showing decline of more than .2 only on high court independence.

Table 6: The Backsliding Process: Judicial Independence, Political and Civil Liberties and Electoral Integrity

Country/Onset of Backsliding Episode and Dates of Reversion	High Court Independence 0,1: always, mostly subservient 2: about half the time 3,4: almost never, never	CSO Repression 0,1: severe, substantial 2: moderate 3,4: weak, none	Media Censorship 0,1: routine 2,3: limited to especially sensitive issues 4: rare	EMB Autonomy 0,1: no, limited autonomy 2: ambiguous 3,4: mostly or entirely autonomous
Liberal democracies: erosion				
Brazil 2016	2015-2019: 3.51 to 3.09 –.42	2015-2019: 3.94 to 2.88 –1.06	2015-2019: 3.82 to 1.92. –1.90	2015-2019: 3.72 to 3.04 –.68
Greece 2017	2016-2017: 3.2 to 2.77 –0.43	2016-2019: 3.88 to 3.81 –.07	2016-2017: 2.74 to 2.65 –.09	2016-2019: 3.72 (no change)
Hungary 2011	2010- 2019: 2.73 to 2.11 –.62	2010-2019: 3.35 to 2.27 –1.08	2010-2018: 3.01 to 2.06 –.95	2010-2018: 3.12 to 2.08 –1.04
Poland 2016	2015-2019: 3.57 to 2.41 –1.16	2015-2019: 3.82 to 2.6 –1.22	2015-2019: 3.84 to 2.02 –1.82	2015-2019: 3.67 to 2.37 –1.3
United States 2016	2015-2019: 3.57 to 3.49 –.08	2015-2019: 3.77 to 3.83 +.06	2015-2019: 3.6 to 3.2 –.4	2015-2019: 3.53 to 3.29 –.24
Electoral Democracy: erosion				
Bolivia 2007	2006-2012: 1.3 to .65 –.65	2006-2015: 3.34 to 2.61 –.73	2006-2019: 2.71 to 1.83 –.87	2006-2019: 3.21 to 1.29 –1.91

Table 6: (cont.)

Dominican Republic 2014	2013-2015: 0.77 to 0.55 −.22	2013-2016: 3.65 to 3.38 −.27	2013-2017: 3.22 to 2.63 −.59	2013-2018: 2.46 to 2.4 −.06
Ecuador 2009	2008-2016: 1.21 to 0.7 −.51	2008-2016: 2.2 to 1.67 −.53	2008-2017: 2.72 to 1.35 −1.37	2008-2016: 2.47 to 2.36 −.11
Electoral democracies: reversion				
Macedonia 2010; reversion 2012-2016	2009-2016: 2.51 to 0.34 −2.17	2009-2016: 3.14 to 2.56 −.58	2009-2012: 1.72 to 1.42 −.3	2009-2014: 2.66 to 2.22 −.44
Nicaragua 2005, reversion 2008-2019	2004-2019: 1.06 to 0.17 −.89	2004-2018: 3.33 to 0.54 −2.79	2004-2019: 3.46 to 0.43 −3.03	2004-2019: 1.65 to 0.49 −1.16
Russia 2000, reversion 2000-2019	1999-2017: 1.35 to 0.16 −1.19	1999-2019: 3.17 to 1.45 −1.72	1999-2019: 2.32 to 0.3 −2.02	1999-2016: 1.97 to .95 −1.02
Serbia 2013, reversion 2017-2019	2012-2017: 2.31 to 1.67 −.63	2012-2016: 2.96 to 2.16 −.8	2012-2018: 1.75 to 0.33 −1.42	2012-2019: 2.79 to 1.6 −1.19
Turkey 2010, reversion 2014-2019	2009-2018: 2.83 to 1.35 −1.48	2009-2017: 2.58 to 0.84 −1.74	2009-2019: 2.28 to 0.41 −1.87	2009-2017: 2.83 to 1.35 −1.48
Ukraine 2010, reversion 2014-2018	2009-2014: 1.74 to 0.91 −.83	2009-2014: 3.4 to 2.58 −.82	2009-2014: 2.93 to 1.73 −1.2	2009-2011: 2.23 to 1.12 −1.11
Venezuela 1998, reversion 2006-2019	1997-2011: 2.39 to 0.15 −2.24	1997-2019: 3.37 to 1.36 −2.01	1997-2018: 2.96 to 0.1 −2.86	1997-2018: 2.89 to 0.24 −2.65
Zambia 2016, reversion 2016-2019	2015-2019:2.33 to 2.13 −.2	2015 to 2019: 3.12 to 2.31 −.81	2015-2016: 1.2 to 0.41 −.79	2015-2019: 2.88 to 1.86 −1.02

or more before indicators bottomed out and the full extent of decline became apparent. In Venezuela, where backsliding dates from 1998, the lowest points in the indicators under Chávez were not registered until 2013, the last year of his life, and they managed to fall to new lows under his successor Nicolás Maduro in 2018–2019.

Declines were relatively modest in several of the liberal democracies (notably, the Dominican Republic, Greece and the United States). But the table also shows quite steep declines in a number of democracies that were once considered consolidated. Prior to the onset of their backsliding episodes, for example, both Hungary and Poland achieved close to the highest possible scores (between 3 and 4) on all of the dimensions assessed in Table 6, with the exception of Hungary's score for high court independence. By 2018–2019, performance on all four measures had been seriously compromised in both countries. Venezuela's scores were lower than Hungary's and Poland's at the onset of its backsliding episode, but they were still higher than the Latin American benchmark at the time. Similarly, Brazil was well above regional benchmarks before democracy began to erode from 2016.

Finally, it is important to underline a point to which we return in more detail: that starting point matters. None of the liberal democracies revert to authoritarian rule. But backsliding in countries that are electoral democracies from the outset are at greater risk of reversion. Of the eleven electoral democracies in the sample, nine had at least one dimension on which their scores registered below 2.0 *before* the onset of the backsliding episodes we have identified; Venezuela and Turkey are the sole exceptions.

4.2 The Causal Effects of Incrementalism

We have defined backsliding as an incremental *process* of derogation from democratic institutions, rules and norms. As argued, the causal effects of incrementalism operate through two postulated mechanisms. First, incremental derogations erode democracy because a weakening of one component of democracy sets the stage for the assault on the next one. Second, behavioral or social-psychological process also come into play. Incrementalism makes it difficult to identify derogations from democratic practice and thus weakens opposition.

We expand on these insights with illustrations from four cases that have served as models of the process: the Venezuelan model of backsliding in Latin America; Putin's establishment of an "electoral autocracy" in Russia; Hungary's "illiberal" democracy; and the United States under Donald Trump.

4.2.1 Venezuela

In Venezuela, the election of Hugo Chávez in 1998 marks the onset of the backsliding episode; as in Section 2, we consider developments starting ten years before the backsliding episode. As Figure 5 shows, the level of democracy did not plateau during the early "frontal assault" period detailed in the last section, particularly 1998–2000; rather, the downward trends continued well into the twenty-first century. Here we focus on how the constitutional and legal ambiguities associated with Chávez's early moves facilitated the further accretion of powers.

Given his history as a military leader who had led an abortive coup six years earlier, Chávez's election naturally raised concerns. The Constitutional Assembly's high-handed assumption of legislative authority was only reluctantly approved by the Supreme Court; its president resigned in protest, arguing that her colleagues "preferred suicide to assassination" (Corrales 2018, 122). But the Court had buckled to pressure from incumbent governments before the rise of Chávez.

Similar ambiguities surrounded the drafting of the new constitution itself. The new powers assumed by Chávez – dissolving the legislature and increasing his control over oil resources, among other things – were promulgated by a duly constituted constituent body. Chávez also acquiesced to some checks on executive authority. Presidential decree powers, for example, remained more limited than in democratic states such as Argentina and Brazil. In addition, the constitution included a provision for

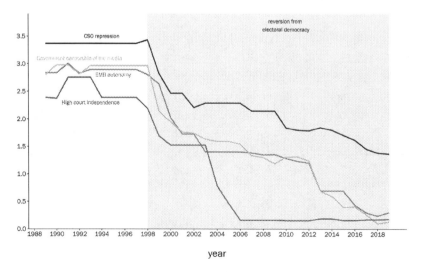

year

Figure 5: Backsliding in Venezuela, 1988–2019.

a recall referendum, which the opposition deployed against Chávez in 2004. Although in retrospect the new Constitution was a clear sign of autocratic intent, this was by no means clear at the time to opponents and to moderate coalition partners.

Between 2001 and 2003, Chávez began to stack formally independent agencies with political loyalists. Resurgent opposition forces responded with massive street protests and general strikes, and in 2002 a coalition of opposition leaders and senior officers temporarily placed Chávez under arrest. But the political forces supporting the coup quickly raised questions about whether the plotters were democrats. Popular and military support for the takeover quickly dissolved after Pedro Carmona, its civilian leader, announced that he would scrap the 1999 constitution, dissolve the legislature and nullify elections to state governorships. It did not help that the United States quickly endorsed the coup. The episode gave credence to Chávez's claim that he, not his opponents, was the true defender of Venezuelan democracy. Chávez used the opportunity to purge the military and rally support from his domestic and international allies, while moderate forces that might have slowed or blocked his ascent were thrown off balance.

Further steps toward the consolidation of Chávez's power followed in quick succession, visible in the declines in all indicators in the 2000–2005 period. In 2002–2003, he faced down a crippling strike in the state oil sector by summarily dismissing 19,000 middle-management and skilled workers and assuming direct control over the management of PDVSA. In 2004, he overcame an attempt to oust him through constitutional channels, deploying a timely upswing in oil revenues to defeat a recall initiative. The opposition's defeat in the oil strikes and in the 2004 referendum marked a turning point in the balance of political power, and Chávez quickly exploited it to further expand his powers. Shortly following the victory in the 2004 referendum, the Chavista congressional majority expanded the size of the Supreme Court from twenty to thirty-two members and filled vacancies with political loyalists. In 2004, legislation issued vague prohibitions against media content that "foments citizens' anxiety" or "disrespects authority," tightening censorship powers.

After the opposition boycott of the 2005 congressional elections, Chávez gained complete control of the legislature, and further restrictions followed. A year later, after eight years of erosion, the Chávez regime fell below our threshold for electoral democracy. Yet Chávez was far from finished. Attacks on the media continued, including the withdrawal of the broadcast license for the country's largest independent channel and the grant of sweeping powers to the National Telecommunications Commission (CONATEL) in 2010. New decree powers also expanded the government's control over education, agriculture, and other key sectors of the economy and increased its control of the electoral machinery.

As the Venezuelan economy plummeted in the mid-2010s, the successor government of Nicolás Maduro relied more heavily on coercion and fraud to stave off the opposition. All four V-Dem indicators continue to trend down following Chávez's death in 2013 – some toward zero – as Venezuela completely unraveled. But in 1998, neither moderate allies nor potential opponents could have foreseen this outcome. Early steps taken under apparently democratic rules and the incremental nature of the process gradually expanded executive powers while throwing the opposition off balance. Only very late in the game were these measures superseded by greater and greater reliance on outright repression.

4.2.2 Russia

Figure 6 replicates the path of the components of democracy in Russia between 1990 and 2019. These scores were low to begin with, reflecting the fragility of liberal institutions under Yeltsin; indeed, there were doubts that Russia had ever really crossed a democratic threshold (Fish 2005).[9] But it is clear that Putin's autocracy did not emerge all at once. Scores declined markedly on all indicators in the 1999–2002 period, the early years of Putin's time in power, and then stabilized. We then see further deterioration when Putin returned to the presidency after a four-year hiatus in 2012.

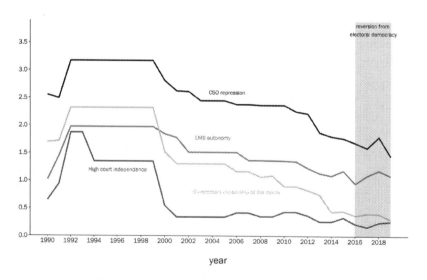

Figure 6: Backsliding in Russia, 1990–2019.

---

[9] See the online Appendix for a more extended discussion of this issue.

From the outset of his first term as president, Putin took a number of steps which – with the benefit of hindsight – appear to have weakened horizontal checks on Putin's power and the prospects for a viable opposition. Independent media was an important early target, visible in the sharp falloff of censorship scores early in his term. In 2000 and 2001, Putin forced the transfer of ownership of NTV – the major independent news channel – from Vladimir Gusinsky to the state-owned Gazprom, reflective of a relentless assault on independent media. Putin pushed through a law in 2002 that allowed the government to suspend parties and NGOs accused of "terrorism," using a national security justification to begin the wider clampdown on civil society that was to follow. Registration and licensing laws increasingly curtailed the role of NGOs and human rights groups, particularly those with foreign funding.

Putin also went after the oligarchs that had gotten fabulously rich from the privatization of the late 1990s. In March 2004, the government launched the prosecution of Mikhail Khodorkovsky, a supporter of the liberal opposition, and forced the sale of Yukos, Khodorkovsky's giant oil and gas company. Other oligarchs were offered the opportunity to trade political power for the right to make money.

A particular focus of the government's attention was to rationalize the complex patchwork of treaties that the Yeltsin government had signed with Russia's own subnational governments. This meant going after the power of the governors. A law pushed through the Duma removed the right of governors to seats in the upper chamber, consolidating Putin's power in the legislature and marking the first step toward elimination of independently elected governors altogether in 2004.

Yet many of Putin's actions could be seen as tough love that would tame the Wild West politics of the 1990s and strengthen a badly weakened state. Indeed, Putin ran on just such a platform, and polls showed overwhelming support. Outsiders as well as Russians remained uncertain about the country's political trajectory. In a book published in 2001, for example, Michael McFaul – later US ambassador to the country, and a persistent critic of Putin – was clear-eyed about the threats posed by his autocratic behavior. Nonetheless, he argued at the time that "no significant actor has a major incentive yet to deviate from existing institutional arrangements of electoralism and constitutionalism" (McFaul 2001, 363). Treisman and Sheleifer (2004, 38) argued Russia has "changed from a communist dictatorship to a multiparty democracy in which officials are chosen in regular elections" and that the abuses evident in the system were no worse than those in other middle-income countries.

It was not until the mid-2000s that the predictions of the pessimists were unambiguously born out. The parliamentary election of December 2003 was an important point in this process. In an uneven contest widely criticized by international observers, Putin's reconstituted party, United Russia, captured two-thirds of the seats in the Duma, giving the president unchecked control over legislation, appointments and even constitutional amendments. In a cabinet reshuffle, Putin proceeded to expand his control over the law enforcement apparatus, expanding the role of loyalists and former KGB officers in high positions within the defense and interior ministries. Constitutional "reforms" expanded the power of the president while weakening the electoral chances of the opposition.

These changes are visible in the declines in scores on the integrity of elections, censorship and judicial autonomy in 2005–2007. In the Freedom House report of 2005, the regime was downgraded from Partly Free to Not Free: "Russians," the report argued, "cannot change their government democratically, particularly in light of the state's far-reaching control of broadcast media and the growing harassment of opposition parties and their financial backers." In 2006, the regime itself formulated and advanced the concept of "sovereign democracy" to distinguish it from Western liberal variants, underlining that the state reflected the interests of the whole nation, a classic majoritarian-nationalist appeal.

As Figure 6 shows, the slide did not stop in the mid-2000s. Democratic decline accelerated again in the early 2010s. The controversial 2011 Duma elections were riddled with irregularities, and in 2012 Putin returned to the presidency. Russia saw a wave of protests over the course of 2011–2012 directed primarily at electoral fraud. These protests were matched by countermobilizations by Putin's supporters and a new law that imposed severe penalties on "illicit" protest. Raids on a number of opposition figures followed; outright repression of opponents became more frequent. The new Putin administration ushered in a wide-ranging assault on civil society organizations and individual rights at its outset: a law against "homosexual propaganda," a law restricting the activities of NGOs receiving foreign funding (and the expulsion of a number of foreign ones) and the recriminalization of slander.

Putin's actions following his return to power are typically associated with the effort to reassert Russia's status abroad, including with respect to Ukraine, Syria and the US presidential election. Yet these were but the foreign face of continuing efforts to stamp out dissent at home. Well into 2019, the administration was still undertaking wide-ranging and coordinated raids on opposition politicians in order to weaken their electoral effectiveness.

Could this incremental slide toward authoritarianism have been stopped in the early years of the Putin era? In hindsight, it appears unlikely. Liberal democratic forces in Russia were disorganized and weak, while – until the late 2000s – Putin's electoral dominance was undergirded by a strong economy and successful nationalist appeals. But although Western judgment about the prospects of Russian democracy was not the main desideratum in its approach toward the country, the ambiguity about the direction of Russia's development did keep Europe and the United States off balance, increasing Putin's room for maneuver vis-à-vis political opponents at home.

4.2.3 Hungary

The onset of backsliding in Hungary dates from the overwhelming victory of Viktor Orbán's Fidesz party in the 2010 parliamentary elections. As shown in Figure 7, an initial inflection following the 2010 elections was followed by the same incremental erosion on all four indicators visible in Venezuela and Russia (Bánkuti, Halmai & Scheppele 2012; Grzymala-Busse 2019).

In Section 3 we reviewed how Fidesz's parliamentary supermajority allowed Orbán to undertake dramatic "reforms" of the judiciary through constitutional amendment, ordinary laws and the power of appointments. It is worth underlining that this process unfolded incrementally, first in the amendment of the Consitution itself in 2011 and subsequently through regular laws that further strengthened Orbán's control and provided legal cover for forced retirements. Judges' ability to resist these reforms was limited given the threat of removal, and retirements resumed after Orbán's reelection in 2018.

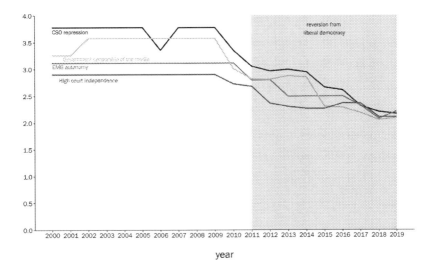

Figure 7: Backsliding in Hungary, 2000–2019.

But the judiciary was hardly his only target. Among the other early steps were a series of electoral "reforms" intended to insure the maintenance of Fidesz's oversized parliamentary majority. Legislation passed in early 2011 undertook complex changes in electoral rules that were difficult for the public to understand: changing the number of members of parliament, drawing new districts and increasing the number of single-member districts. The law also extended voting rights to pro-Fidesz ethnic expatriates in neighboring countries while making it harder for diasporas elsewhere in Europe and the United States to vote. (Orenstein, Krekó Juhász 2015). As Figure 8 shows, the independence of election monitoring deteriorates in a step-wise fashion in the run-up to the 2018 elections, which FIDESZ won resoundingly despite charges of fraud and abuse.

Incremental encroachments are also visible in the sphere of the media, civil society, and individual rights and liberties. Orbán almost immediately placed pressure on independent media outlets and on civil society organizations. Shortly following the 2010 elections, the government withdrew advertising to commercial media outlets and required them to register with a regulatory agency empowered to fine or even revoke licenses for infractions (Freedom House 2016a). Independent news and advertising outlets were pressed to sell out to Orbán cronies or were forced out of business. Publishers and journalists did not initially face threats of imprisonment or physical assaults as was the case in Russia. As in Venezuela, however, they have been threatened with penalties for publishing content that is not "balanced, accurate, thorough, objective, and responsible" (Kelemen 2017, 12).

Registration and auditing requirements were also increasingly deployed to harass civil society groups. NGOs and other organizations with financial ties to George Soros, the liberal Hungarian-American billionaire, were an easy target, and in 2016 and 2017 the government initiated a campaign to drive the prestigious Central European University out of Hungary. But the net swept up a wider variety of civil society groups working on the rights of women, the LGBT community, refugees and migrants, and the rule of law.

Finally, Hungary also exemplifies the way autocrats can serve their interest in political polarization by attacks on the rights of vulnerable communities who are demonized as "the other." The government has generally turned a blind eye to hate crimes committed against the Roma minority, sometimes with the collaboration of Jobbik or even Fidesz politicians themselves (Cernusakova 2017). Migrants suffered official detention and even more violent abuse, and in 2018 the government began to press for financial penalties against civil society organizations coming to their aid (Kingsley 2018). The 2018 election saw an uptick in xenophobic rhetoric.

To what extent – and through what mechanisms – can these incremental steps be depicted as a self-reinforcing process? Orbán capitalized on the cultural and economic resentments of rural and small-town voters, and there is little doubt that Fidesz's parliamentary supermajority cleared the way for subsequent abuses of power. But the nominally legal and gradual character of the backsliding process itself was an essential element. Because Hungarian backsliding was "softer" than the murder of members of the opposition and journalists in Russia or the repression of demonstrations in Venezuela, the country remained above the democratic threshold in both our dataset and most others; it was not until 2019 that Freedom House downgraded the regime from "Free" to "Partly Free." And for all the abuses that permeated Orbán's "illiberal democracy," the absence of outright coercion, threats and police repression provided a cover for the tolerance on the part of other EU members who otherwise might have served as an external check on the regime (Kelemen 2019); we return to this international context in more detail in the Conclusion.

4.2.4 Trump's America

The steps toward democratic erosion under Donald Trump are more difficult to pinpoint, in part because Trump's time in office is still relatively short in comparative terms (three years as of this writing). The overall changes in the indicators that do deteriorate begin from a much higher level than in the other cases we consider and are more subtle (Figure 8). The two indicators that actually shift – with respect to election management and media censorship – do so before Trump's election, although his assault on the media is reflected in a sharp downturn on that variable after his election. The integrity of the electoral system also drifts down, but partly reflecting concerns at the state level where elections are ultimately managed. Although the United States does show a significant shift in the country's V-Dem liberal democracy scores, a consideration of the four indicators we track here could lead to the sanguine conclusion that nothing much has ultimately changed. Horizontal checks remain robust, civil society and individual rights remain protected, and the integrity of the electoral system remains largely intact.

But this judgment would clearly be mistaken. The effort to expand presidential prerogatives and to weaken legislative, judicial and administrative checks on his behavior has clearly been the most contentious feature of the Trump presidency. The penchant for executive orders during his first year, the early war with the FBI and Justice Department, and manifest conflicts of interests with respect to Trump's businesses all served to signal Trump's expansive views of executive prerogative. Some of these actions – most notably the travel

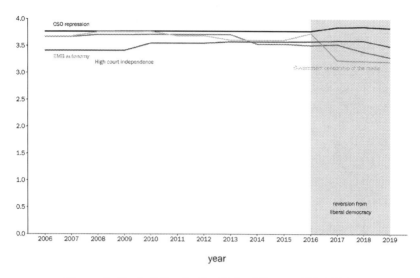

Figure 8: Backsliding in the United States, 2006–2019.

ban – ultimately had to be modified in the face of legal challenge. Others, such as the use of a declaration of national emergency to divert Congress-authorized military spending to the border wall, remain tied up in the courts as this is being written. Nonetheless these measures signaled a willingness to stretch the limits of presidential power.

The issue of horizontal checks on the president initially crystallized around the Russia probe and the relationship between the executive, the Department of Justice and the federal law enforcement apparatus. The firing of FBI Director James Comey and Trump's complaints about Attorney General Jeff Session's recusal set a combative tone. Continuous attacks on the Mueller probe clearly sought to delegitimate the inquiry. When the Mueller report was finally released, the interpretation of it offered by Trump's second attorney general, William Barr, did not accurately comport with the contents of the report – particularly with respect to possible obstruction charges – raising concerns that the attorney general was acting as the president's personal advocate. In May 2019, Trump sought to assert executive privilege with respect to the report and all underlying materials. His assertions of privilege expanded dramatically in response to the Ukraine inquiry, pushing crucial constitutional issues onto the courts and – as a result – also stalling investiga-tive processes.

The judiciary, as well as Congress and the Department of Justice, were also targets of presidential attack. When a circuit court ruled against his immigration policy, the president characterized the decision as a "lawless disgrace," with hints of retaliation against the judiciary. The episode triggered a highly unusual public assertion of judicial independence on the part of the chief justice of the Supreme Court himself.

Similar norm-breaking is evident in the shift in the nature of political discourse with respect to rights and the media. Trump's campaign appealed to white identity politics and his denigration of racial, ethnic and other vulnerable minorities mainstreamed radical ideas that were once on the fringe of American politics (Neiwert 2017). Of particular significance in this regard are his attacks on immigrants (a purposely ambiguous term that includes both naturalized citizens as well as the undocumented), his charged response to Charlottesville, initiatives vis-à-vis the LGBT communities such as the ability of transgender citizens to serve in the military, and his support for a militarized response to the 2020 protests following the death of George Floyd. The corresponding increase in hate crimes has been widely documented and goes directly to the question of the protection of rights and liberties (Southern Poverty Law Center 2019). But because it is impossible to establish precise causal connections between bad words and bad deeds, it is difficult for Trump's critics to hold him and his political allies directly accountable.

Trump's rhetorical attacks on the press – "fake news," "enemies of the people" – is unprecedented in the United States, as is his practice of calling out specific networks and even individual journalists for intimidating criticism. As in the other cases of backsliding, unrelenting recourse to the "big lie" has contributed to the growing confusion about, or indifference to, verifiable facts; these issues became particularly visible following the outbreak of the pandemic in early 2020. Although the media has fought back, the long-term economic difficulties faced by network television and print journalism have increased their vulnerability to such pressures (Anderson Jones & West 2017).

Similar norm- and even law-breaking extends to the integrity of the electoral system itself. The effort to restrict voting rights came from Republican allies in state legislatures, rather than directly from the executive (although the president did set up a Presidential Advisory Commission on Electoral Integrity, which was subsequently disbanded). But the president's own interest in tilting the playing field was indicated by disinterest in Russian election meddling, potential obstruction of the Mueller probe and his effort to enlist Ukrainian President Zelensky in an investigation of his most prominent Democratic presidential challenger, Joe Biden.

To what extent did the ambiguities of Trump's first three years in power enable increasing abuses over time? As suggested in Section 3, the acquiescence of congressional Republicans to these abuses has been a pivotal factor in the American backsliding process. It loomed especially large as the Democratic majority in the House of Representatives voted for articles of impeachment over Trump's efforts to enlist Ukrainian assistance in the 2020 presidential elections. In response, the Senate leadership stated openly that they planned to coordinate strategy with the White House, a perfect example of the collapse in the separation of powers.

Would Republican resistance to Trump's behavior have been stronger if the Ukranian scandal had erupted earlier in the presidential term? There are obviously no clear answers to these questions. And it should be emphasized that, from the very onset of the Trump presidency, deep partisan divisions – and especially fear of primary election defeats – provided a strong disincentive for congressional Republicans to push back against executive overreach. Even so, there are good reasons to believe that the "normalization" of abuses enhanced the president's ability to rally Republican support against impeachment and other efforts at oversight. Partisan antipathy was already high at the onset of Trump's term but became even more intense and more personal by 2019 (Pew Research Center 2019). Increasing polarization, in turn, has worked to strengthen the appeal of the "deep state" concept, with the most basic legal and administrative processes increasingly brought into the ambit of political competition.

With increasing polarization, Republican incentives to challenge the president have became even weaker, especially as the ranks of the congressional moderates thinned. In 2017, House Republicans continued to warn against presidential interference with the Mueller report; by 2018, they dismissed the report's detailed evidence of obstruction of justice; and by 2019, they held the line against the transparent use of presidential power against his political opponents in the Ukraine scandal. The outcome of the impeachment controversy of 2019 was a foregone conclusion. But the partisan divide in Congress clearly deepened the constitutional crisis generated by the president's defiance of a legitimate constitutional inquiry, and it is likely to deal lasting damage to American democracy regardless of the outcome.

4.2.5 Incrementalism: A Reprise

More definitive claims about the role of incrementalism in the backsliding process would require a more comprehensive examination of the timing of the introduction of different measures and the relationship among them. Case study work can explore counterfactuals about when and how oppositions might have been able to block abuses of power. The preceding sketches do, however, suggest that we should take seriously the hypothesis that backsliding has "slippery slope" qualities. In each case, early derogations – particularly the removal of horizontal checks bolstered by majoritarian justifications – set the stage for further derogations and in three cases the decline of democracy itself. In each case, backsliding advanced because of the legally ambiguous nature of the actions in question, their incrementalism and the corresponding difficulty for oppositions to coalesce to counter them.

4.3 Backsliding within Democracies and Transitions to Competitive Authoritarian Regimes

As noted in Section 1, we distinguish between erosion – backsliding that remains within democratic bounds – and outright reversion to authoritarian rule. Under what conditions does backsliding cross the line into competitive authoritarianism? Under what conditions does the process stop short?

We identify reversions as any case in which backsliding leads to a decline below 0.5 on the V-Dem Electoral Democracy Index (EDI), a threshold others have used as well (Lührmann, Tannenberg & Lindberg 2018, 6). While arbitrary, the EDI puts particular weight on bedrock features of democracy: that regimes hold free and fair elections for executive office, with multiparty competition, and a minimum of guarantees with respect to freedom of association and expression. Table 7 revisits information provided in Section 1 and in the online Appendix by dividing our cases into four possible cells: backsliding that occurs *within* democracies that are either liberal or electoral; and backsliding from either liberal or electoral democracy to authoritarian rule. A first, critical point to note is that the liberal democracy–reversion cell is empty. At the time of this writing, none of the five regimes classified as liberal democracies had slipped into competitive authoritarianism, although Hungary did finally fall below the V-Dem democratic threshold in the revised 2020 version of the dataset (v.10).

The relative resilience of liberal democracies is good news. It suggests that crossing certain institutional threshholds captured by the liberal democracy index would provide inoculation against backsliding all the way to authoritarian rule. In highly institutionalized democracies, political actors invest heavily in skills and resources required to play by the rules of the game and have deep stakes in maintaining them. In such systems, horizontal checks, robust political rights and liberties, and free and fair election processes reinforce one another and constrain executive malfeasance.

The United States is the case in our sample in which democratic institutions were strongest and most long-lived. Although we have presented evidence that the Trump presidency has weakened American democracy, it is doubtful that the United States will revert to competitive authoritarian rule. Trump's approach to politics violated a number of conventional norms, but many attempted

Table 7: Backsliding and Reversion in Electoral and Liberal Democracies

	Backsliding/No Reversion	Reversion
Liberal Democracy	Brazil 2016-2019 Greece 2017-2019 Hungary 2011-2019 Poland 2016-2019 United States 2016-2019	
Electoral Democracy	Bolivia 2007-2019 Dominican Republic 2014-2018 Ecuador 2009-2017	Macedonia erosion from 2010, reversion from 2012-2016. Nicaragua erosion from 2005; reversion 2008-2019. Russia, reversion 2000-2019. Serbia erosion from 2013, reversion 2017-2019. Turkey, erosion from 2010, reversion 2014-2019. Ukraine, erosion from 2010, reversion 2014-2019 Venezuela, erosion from 1998; reversion 2006-2019 Zambia, reversion 2016-2019

derogations encountered strong headwinds: from the judiciary, from the media, from civil society and – from 2019 – from the newly empowered Democratic majority in the House of Representatives. Whatever damage Trump's presidency might have done to American democracy, it did not take the form of a fundamental change in political regime.

In contrast, backsliding in eight of the eleven electoral democracies did eventually decline into competitive authoritarianism. And two of the three regimes in the electoral democracy category (Bolivia and Ecuador) are marginal cases where a judgment of reversion is arguably warranted. These findings bolster the observation made in the Introduction, and supported by other literature that the democracies most at risk of reversion are those that are more weakly institutionalized to begin with. The electoral democracies in our sample were generally much younger and lacked the horizontal checks or the political and social organizations to push back against executive overreach. As a result, not only were horizontal checks and political rights at risk but the integrity of electoral institutions was ultimately vulnerable to executive encroachment as well. In all of the regimes that reverted to competitive authoritarianism, pliant legislatures and weak courts acquiesced or looked the other way as illiberal executives intimidated political oppositions, filled electoral agencies with partisan loyalists, and engaged in corruption and outright fraud that fundamentally tilted the electoral playing field against effective opposition.

Table 8 provides more disaggregated evidence that institutional starting points affect whether or not backsliding leads to regime change. The table shows the average scores for liberal and electoral democracies in the year preceding the onset of the backsliding episodes for each of the democratic pillars displayed in Table 6: high court independence, the autonomy of electoral authorities, civil society and media freedom. Those cases starting as electoral democracies are again divided into those that erode but remain democratic and those that revert to authoritarian rule.

Table 8: Average V-Dem Scores in Year Preceding Onset of Backsliding (Liberal and Electoral Democracies)

	High Court Independence (average)	Civil Society Freedom (average)	Media Freedom (average)	Electoral Authority (average)
Liberal Democracies (Brazil,Greece, Hungary, Poland, United States)	3.56	3.80	3.35	3.25
Electoral Democracies: Reversions (Macedonia, Nic, Russia,Serbia, Turkey,Ukraine, Venezuela, Zambia)	2.25***	2.59**	2.60*	2.26***
Electoral Democracies: Non-Reversions. Bolivia, DR, Ecuador)	2.19***	2.64	2.90	1.20

t-test: difference with Liberal Democracy: *p<0.05 **p<0.01 *** p<0.001

Not surprisingly, almost all of the liberal backsliders had high scores on all the components of democracy that we consider here. Point estimates were near the top of the 4-point scale on all of the dimensions, with overall averages ranging from 3.32 for high court independence to 3.75 for civil society freedom. Hungary, it should be noted, was a partial exception to this pattern: it was the only liberal democracy in which the assessment of high court independence fell below a score of 3.0, and although assessments were above that threshold on all of the other dimensions, its scores were somewhat lower than those of other liberal democracies. Significantly, as noted it was also the only liberal democracy that eventually slipped below the democratic threshold. But in all of the cases – even Hungary – politicians seeking to undermine democracy confronted relatively strong institutions and civil societies at the onset of the backsliding episode.

Electoral democracies, which account for all of the outright reversions, began from far weaker starting points on all of the components of democracy; in these systems, the commitment to democracy on the part of major actors were more tentative and trust among the competitors more limited (Haggard & Kaufman 2016; Mainwaring and Pérez-Liñán 2014). The weakness of the electoral democracies is particularly evident with respect to horizontal checks. Of the eleven electoral democracies, none had a score on the independence of the high court that exceeded 3.0; Turkey, at 2.83, had the highest score.

Perhaps most telling are scores with respect to electoral institutions. Among the eleven electoral democracies only one – Bolivia – scored above 3.0 on the autonomy of electoral monitoring bodies.

Of all of the reverters, Venezuela appeared to have the most robust democratic institutions, which helps explain the prolonged nature of the backsliding process. By 1997, its political institutions had already been shaken by two decades of economic deterioration and political alienation. Even so, its score for civil society (3.37) was roughly on a par with those for the liberal democracies, and those for press freedom and electoral autonomy implied at least moderate conformity with liberal democratic norms. But the assessment of high court autonomy – scored at 2.37 – indicated significant weakness in this core feature of liberal democracy. In fact, as we have discussed in Section 3 and in the online Appendix, the court did buckle to political pressure relatively frequently, and this vulnerability helped pave the way for Chávez's campaign for constitutional reforms in 1999.

It is beyond the scope of this analysis to explain how the three other weak democracies in our sample were able to avoid a slide into outright authoritarianism. If anything, they had even weaker horizontal institutions of accountability than the electoral democracies that *did* revert. Electoral institutions were highly vulnerable to incumbent control in the Dominican Republic and

Ecuador, and in all three countries, the high court was particularly subservient. Civil society organizations did score highly in Bolivia and the Dominican Republic; and although scores were lower in Ecuador, militant indigenous groups and social movements might have provided a deterrent to outright regime change. Unlike Chávez, moreover, neither Evo Morales nor Rafael Correa could exercise full control over the grassroots movements that helped bring them to power (see Table 3, column 4).

However, we again need to underline that the precise definition of democratic thresholds is not only arbitrary but particularly problematic in marginal democracies where incumbents do not operate strictly within democratic limits to begin with. Bolivia, Ecuador, the Dominican Republic and the Philippines – a near-miss backsliding case under Duterte – did not become authoritarian by our metric. But these judgments are subject to significant margins of error, and all might rightly be seen as competitive authoritarian regimes. Bolivia has been identified by the Economic Intelligence Unit as a "hybrid regime" and became more authoritarian after the resignation of Morales in November 2019. Before Rafael Correa's decision not to run for a fourth term, Ecuador fell below a Polity score of 6 in 2006, the conventional threshold for democracy in that data set (see online Appendix narratives on Bolivia and Ecuador).

The problem of identifying a tipping point is closely related to our discussion of the causal role of incrementalism. Hungary, one of our liberal democracy cases, has experienced a "softer," less overtly coercive form of erosion than we see in Latin America or other parts of Eastern Europe. This fact may itself have influenced perceptions that the country remained a democracy; notwithstanding Orbán's illiberalism, most datasets, including our own, support this conclusion, at least until very recently.

But this conclusion may be misleading, even dangerously so. The Orbán regime did not arrest political opponents, physically intimidate voters or prohibit party competition, allowing it to preserve the veneer of democracy. But it had a long history of rigging the political system through constitutional "reforms" that centralized power, as well as through corruption, gerrymandering and the manipulation of the media. Poland has already moved along a similar path (Fomina & Kucharczyk 2016), and we cannot dismiss the possibility that these forms of incremental reversion might become increasingly common among other relatively advanced democratic regimes as well. Barely surviving as a liberal democracy should not be considered an accomplishment but rather a reminder of the risks that face both liberal and electoral democracies.

4.4 Conclusion

Three important conclusions emerge from this discussion of the incremental nature of backsliding. As we noted in the Introduction, the risks of backsliding to outright authoritarian rule are clearly greatest in democracies that are weakly institutionalized to begin with – where political actors are unsure that others will respect the democratic rules of the game. That said, a second finding is that liberal democratic regimes are by no means immune from this process, even if the shifts are more subtle and difficult to trace. Backsliding is not a phenomenon limited to new democracies but is visible in the United States; it has also occurred in countries such as Hungary and Poland that were once considered immune from reversion as a result of their membership in the European Union and solid middle-income status.

Our third and most important point, however, is that the very difficulty of identifying derogations, and autocrats' skill at obfuscation and misdirection, are potentially crucial causal factors in the backsliding process. As we have defined backsliding, the starting point is a democratic context. The incremental departures from democratic norms and the testing of institutional constraints thus enjoy support. But formal institutional and legal shifts – albeit incremental – gradually reshape the political landscape to the advantage of incumbents.

We have also emphasized the social psychology of incrementalism. The very ambiguity of the signals contained in autocratic strategies are difficult for publics to recognize as existential threats to democracy. Oppositions – alert to the dangers – run the risk of being accused of hysteria or crying wolf, and precisely for that reason incremental steps become more difficult to stop. By the time outright legal changes are made, the public has been "softened" or acclimated to new norms, including through control of the media. As we will show in Section 5, these social psychological effects may also operate with respect to outside actors that might otherwise serve to check the backsliding process.

5 Conclusion

Backsliding constitutes a distinctive form of political change. Rather than coups or other frontal assaults on democratic rule, voters have empowered autocrats. These rulers exploit polarization and compliant parties and legislatures to incrementally chip away at the foundations of liberal democratic rule: horizontal checks on executive power; political and civil liberties and ultimately free and fair elections.

We approached backsliding as a complex causal process involving political polarization, the ceding of powers by both voters and legislatures, and a step-by-step attack on institutions and norms. Rather than iterating our findings, we use this Conclusion to briefly consider two additional factors that are garnering more critical attention in understanding these processes: the international context; and the role that information—and disinformation–plays in backsliding and autocracy more generally. The latter of these two issues goes to an even more profound question of the social psychological underpinnings of liberal democratic rule: whether democracy can survive in a post-truth world.

5.1 The International Context: Autocratic Challengers, Erosion in the Core

Our account in this volume focused largely on domestic political dynamics. Global forces are also at work, however, and operating through two channels. Autocratic regimes do not only operate on their home turfs, but have shown a growing interest in protecting authoritarian incumbents and even spreading their political models abroad (Diamond, Plattner and Walker 2016; Tansey 2016; Diamond 2019). At the same time the advanced industrial democracies are themselves vulnerable, and thus less likely to act as ballast for the liberal order; this is particularly true with respect to the United States under Trump (for example, Cooley and Nexon 2020).

The end of the Cold War was initially seen as an unambiguous win for democracy. But beginning with the democratic recession of the mid-2000s, liberal democracy was forced onto the defensive. Not only did the democratizing trend slow, but autocratic states became more prominent players on the global stage. Most notable in this regard were the rise of China as a great power, the resurgence of Russian nationalism and the pernicious effect of Saudi Arabia, other Gulf states and Iran on political developments in the Muslim world. With the possible exception of Russia, which we identify as a backsliding case, these countries were never democratic. Nonetheless, they increasingly projected their favored political models in their neighborhoods and even globally.

China projected its power in the first instance through the steady diversification of its economic ties, most notably in the Belt and Road Initiative, and through its growing influence in international organizations. The Chinese-dominated Asian Infrastructure Investment Bank had significant Western participation, but the Shanghai Cooperation Organization (SCO) grouped China, Russia and a cluster of largely authoritarian regimes in Central Asia around shared security objectives, including dampening political challengers. China also gained sway in multilateral institutions, for example, pushing back on the United Nations human rights machinery.

Russia is a far weaker economic pole than China. Nonetheless, it has leveraged its ample energy reserves, weapons sales, economic ties and outright military intervention to influence developments not only in Central Asia, but in the Middle East and swing states such as Turkey and Serbia. Like China, it has also operated through a parallel universe of authoritarian international institutions such as the Eurasian Economic Union. Even more than China, moreover, Russia has engaged in outright subversion—for example in Georgia and Ukraine–and efforts to weaken the political and social cohesion of democracy in Western Europe and the United States.

The Middle East has long constituted a swath of the world's territory populated largely by authoritarian regimes, and the failure of the Arab Spring to take root had multiple causes that take us far beyond our focus on backsliding. Nonetheless, both Iran and Saudi Arabia have had pernicious political effects, from support of militias and political forces such as Hezbollah and Hamas to the funding of extremist clerics and madrasas. In the case of Saudi Arabia, these influences have reached well beyond the Middle East into South and Southeast Asia and Africa as well.

In addition to the sheer material power wielded by these major authoritarian powers, we should not underestimate ideational appeals and the emergence of a significant anti-liberal counter-narrative (Cooley 2015). A hallmark of the Chinese model, albeit disingenuous, was the promise of non-intervention in internal affairs. In fact, China's version of "authoritarian capitalism" (Foa 2018) had both political and economic resonance, creating a space for models of governance at odds with liberal democratic ones.

These cases were authoritarian from the outset, but backsliding subsequently added to the chorus of illiberal voices. Chávez provided a distinctive political blueprint which included constituent assemblies, new constitutions, demonization of opposition political forces, anti-Americanism and populist redistributive appeals. Left populist models ebbed in Latin America after the end of the commodity boom of the 2000s, but for well over a decade, the Venezuelan model anchored the populist end of Latin America's "pink tide." Orbán's version of illiberal democracy has played a comparable – and still enduring – role in Central Europe, creating particular challenges to the EU (Kelemen 2019; Vachudova 2020). How will an increasingly-divided European Union respond to more-or-less open derogations from liberal democratic rule?

Although no country in the democratic core of the international system has experienced a full authoritarian reversion, it is fair to say that the political systems of the advanced industrial states are under greater threat than at any time since the 1930s (Przeworski 2019), with profound implications for democracy in the rest of the world. At the broadest level, these processes have weakened the institutional foundations of the postwar liberal order. A wide array of institutions from NATO to the WTO and European Union, have come under stress as a result of illiberal leaders and parties. For example, between the waning of the Cold War and the rise of Trump, the American government viewed support for democratic change as consistent with its geopolitical interests as well as with its values. This orientation changed sharply under the Trump administration. Not only have we seen a decline in the democracy promotion and human rights agendas but an open presidential embrace of authoritarian leaders. These include not only backsliders like Orbán and Duterte, but "hard" autocrats such as Putin, Xi Jinping and even Kim Jong Un.

Europe faces somewhat different challenges, as far-right and anti-system parties have with few exceptions not actually been part of ruling coalitions. Nonetheless, they influence the tenor of debate and leaders such as Orbán now sit at the European table. He has aggressively sought to blunt European influence with respect to democracy while simultaneously cutting side-deals with more openly autocratic states including Russia and China (Meunier and Vachudova 2018).

Developments in the United States and Europe have also badly damaged the international image of liberal democracy; the problem of dysfunctionality that we highlighted in Chapter Two is visible abroad as well as at home. Despite its flaws, Western democracy was a model with powerful global resonance and provided a legitimating rationale for democratic reforms throughout the world; as Francis Fukuyama (1989) famously noted, there were no ideological alternatives. Rising authoritarian powers have been quick to challenge that presumption, and the study of the international forces supporting or impeding democracy is likely to grow (Tansey 2016).

5.2 The Social Psychology of Democratic Rule: Can Democracy Survive in a Post-Truth World?

In Section 4, we highlighted the role that freedom of the media played in the backsliding process, and essentially portrayed censorship effort as akin to removing a check on the executive. Yet the broader information environment and the role of social media in backsliding has begun to receive more attention. The reasons are profound and include a growing skepticism about the Enlightenment presumptions about the social and epistemic foundations of democratic rule.

In *Democracy for Realists: Why Elections Do Not Produce Responsive Government,* Christopher Achen and Larry Bartels (2016) summarize this growing skepticism. In contrast to models of the rational voter, most citizens are preoccupied with other pursuits, and do not expend much intellectual energy on politics; their political belief systems are generally "thin, disorganized and ideologically incoherent" (Achen and Bartels 2016, 12). They do not follow the details of even the most salient policy issues, do not fully understand what parties stand for, and vote for candidates and parties who hold positions quite divergent from their own. Rather, deeply held group identities, "tribal affiliations," play an outsized role in political behavior (and probably among those who continue to believe in Enlightenment democratic values as well as their communitarian detractors). These affiliations include ethnic, racial, religious, occupational or local loyalties. Political campaigns, Achen and Bartels conclude, are not exercises in rational persuasion; rather they "consist in large part of reminding voters of their partisan identities— "mobilizing" them to support their group at the polls" (Achen and Bartels 2016, 311). As a result, emotion rather than rational deliberation plays an outsize role in politics.

We can see how this somewhat cynical view of democracy fits with the model of backsliding that we have articulated at all three phases of the process. First, autocrats are master polarizers, and they foment divisions in part by exaggerations and outright falsehoods about the intentions of their adversaries: the elites and other nefarious forces that stand in the way of the popular will (Pomerantsev 2019). Propaganda has always played a central role in autocracy, not only by screening voices critical of the regime but by demonizing the "enemies of the people." Social media makes these appeals easier by permitting a flood of unvetted misinformation. Misinformation—and disinformation— undermines political discourse based on facts and universally understood standards of evidence (O'Connor and Weatherall 2019).

Even in democracies, the very business model of the companies that run social media platforms prevents them from standing up against these processes. Moreover, these strategies exploit deep liberal commitments to free speech and are thus difficult to check. In backsliding cases, autocrats and their allies control the media in ways that make such information silos even deeper. As we now know, these domestic processes are compounded by foreign actors like Russia through astute agenda-setting, framing and targeting of particularly susceptible voters (Jamieson 2018; Sunstein 2018b).

We have shown how autocrats use parties, the legislature and the law to achieve their aims from the top down, evading the institutional checks that are supposed to constrain executives. Here, too, control over information plays a crucial role. Intimidation, or outright control, of the media permits messaging to support backsliding initiatives while drowning out or suppressing opposition voices.

Information control plays a particularly pivotal role in the backsliding process that we elaborate in Section 4, but goes far beyond censorship as traditionally conceived. When autocrats undertake derogations from democratic rule, they do so precisely by exploiting both bias and inattention, incrementally moving their base—and the wider public–toward positions which, in retrospect, mark significant departures from democratic norms. The study of propaganda—long a mainstay of authoritarian regimes—is back as an object of study in liberal democracies as well (for example, Stanley 2015). Control over information, whether centralized or through the proliferation of siloed, hyper-partisan sources, has the effect of obfuscation and the creation of ambiguities that aid the autocrat.

We now have ample evidence from a variety of cases about how social media abetted anti-liberal campaigns, again, not simply through foreign interference but by savvy manipulation and targeting of vulnerable voters by autocrats and other illiberal political forces (for example, Pomerantsev 2019 on middle income countries; Jamieson 2018 on the US). Guriev and Treisman (2019) have gone so far as to call this new generation of backsliding regimes "informational autocracies." They note how astute leaders manufacture support and diffuse dissent by plying messages stressing performance and attentiveness to citizen need, while relying less on outright coercion and violence. A post-truth world is not only damaging for individuals, who may be induced to act in self-destructive ways by the deluge of misinformation they are exposed to on a daily basis. The absence of epistemological anchors also threatens to unwind the basic premises of rational discourse, debate and contestation on which democratic rule ultimately rests.

5.3 By Way of Conclusion

As this Element was being finalized, the world faced the outbreak of the most significant global pandemic since the great influenza of 1918. As we noted in passing in Chapter One, profound crises can provide plausible reasons for democratic governments to accept tradeoffs with respect to executive powers and even individual freedoms; this is true in war and civil war, in the face of terrorism, and in response to large-scale ecological or health disasters such as COVID-19 as well. Balancing these tradeoffs is an ongoing issue in any democracy, but the risks of erosion – or even reversion – are real. National crises offer opportunities for illiberal rulers to tighten their grip on power. In Hungary, for example, Viktor Orbán quickly assumed virtually unlimited decree powers in response to the COVID-19 outbreak, casting off even the semblance of democratic government.

The foregoing reflections on the role of international forces, the information environment, the social psychological foundations of democracy and the role of crises are ultimately linked. As global developments trend toward greater nationalism and tribalism, the processes we have identified are increasingly wrapped up in the international correlation of forces, foreign policy considerations and transnational risks.

Complacency plays a critical role in the backsliding process, as oppositions and publics are lulled into accepting autocratic messaging and a subtly shifting status quo. These risks are compounded in times of crisis such as that unleashed by COVID-19. Incremental erosion is an ever-present danger even in the most robust democracies. Studying its causes and effects—conceptualizing, modeling, measuring and telling stories—is not just an academic exercise. Understanding such processes is crucial to the defense of democracy itself.

References

Abrajano, Marisa, and Zoltan L. Hajnal. 2017. *White Backlash: Immigration, Race, and American Politics*. Princeton, NJ: Princeton University Press.

Abramowitz, Alan I., and Steven Webster. 2016. "The rise of negative partisanship and the nationalization of US elections in the 21st Century." *Electoral Studies* 41(March): 12–22.

Acemoglu, Daron, and James A. Robinson. 2006. *Economic Origins of Dictatorship and Democracy*. New York: Cambridge University Press.

Achen, Christopher, and Larry Bartels. 2016. *Democracy for Realists: Why Elections Do Not Produce Responsive Government*. Princeton, NJ: Princeton University Press.

Albright, Madeleine. 2018. *Fascism: A Warning*. New York: Harper.

Anderson Jones, Robbell, and Sonja R. West. 2017. "Don't expect the first amendment to protect the media." *New York Times*, January 25.

Armingeon, Klaus, and Kai Guthman. 2014. "Democracy in crisis: The declining support for national democracy in European countries, 2007–2011." *European Journal of Political Research* 53(3): 423–442.

Autor, David, David Dorn, Gordon Hanson, and Kaveh Majlesi. 2017. "Importing political polarization? The electoral consequences of rising trade exposure." National Bureau of Economic Research Working Paper No. 22637 (December). Cambridge: National Bureau of Economic Research. www.nber.org/papers/w22637 (accessed October 3, 2020).

Bánkuti, Miklós, Gábor Halmai, and Kim Lane Scheppele. 2012. "Hungary's illiberal turn: Disabling the constitution." *Journal of Democracy* 23(3): 138–146

Bermeo, Nancy. 2016. "On democratic backsliding." *Journal of Democracy* 27 (1): 5–19.

Boix, Carles. 2003. *Democracy and Redistribution*. New York: Cambridge University Press.

Capoccia, Giovanni. 2005. *Defending Democracy: Reactions to Extremism in Interwar Europe*. Baltimore, MD: Johns Hopkins University Press.

Carothers, Thomas. 2002. "The end of the transition paradigm." *Journal of Democracy* 13(1): 5–21.

Carothers, Thomas, and Andrew O'Donohue, eds. 2019. *Democracies Divided: The Global Challenge of Political Polarization*. Washington, DC: The Brookings Institution.

Cernusakova, Barbora. 2017. "The Roma people's Hungarian hell: A ruling by the European Court of Human Rights highlights the pattern of persecution." *Politico*, January 25. www.politico.eu/article/the-roma-peoples-hungarian-hell/ (accessed October 3, 2020).

Cooley, Alexander. 2015. "Authoritarianism goes global: Countering democratic norms." *Journal of Democracy* 26(3): 49–63.

Cooley, Alexander, and Daniel Nexon. 2020. *Exit from Hegemony: The Unraveling of the American Global Order.* New York: Oxford University Press.

Coppedge, Michael, et. al. 2019. *V-Dem Dataset v9*, Varieties of Democracy (V-Dem) Project. https://doi.org/10.23696/vdemcy19 (accessed October 3, 2020).

Corrales, Javier. 2018. *Fixing Democracy: Why Constitutional Change Often Fails to Enhance Democracy in Latin America.* New York: Oxford University Press.

Crozier, Michel, Samuel P. Huntington, and Joji Watanuki. 1975. *The Crisis of Democracy.* New York: New York University Press.

Diamond, Larry. 2002. "Elections without democracy: Thinking about hybrid regimes." *Journal of Democracy* 13(2): 21–35.

  2015. "Facing up to the democratic recession." *Journal of Democracy* 26(1): 141–155.

  2019. *Ill Winds: Saving Democracy from Russian Rage, Chinese Ambition and American Complacency.* New York: Penguin.

Diamond, Larry, and Leonardo Morlino. 2004. "The quality of democracy: An overview." *Journal of Democracy* 15(4): 20–31.

Diamond, Larry, Marc F. Plattner, and Christopher Walker. 2016. *Authoritarianism Goes Global: The Challenge to Democracy.* Baltimore, MD: Johns Hopkins University Press.

Eatwell, Roger, and Matthew Goodwin. 2018. *National Populism: The Revolt against Democracy.* New York: Penguin.

Economist Intelligence Unit. 2020. Democracy Index 2019. www.eiu.com/topic/democracy-index (accessed January 8, 2020).

Eichengreen, Barry. 2018. *The Populist Temptation: Economic Grievance and Political Reaction in the Modern Era.* New York: Oxford University Press.

Elster, Jon and Rune Slagstad, eds. 1988. *Constitutionalism and Democracy.* Cambridge. Cambridge University Press.

Fiorina, Morris. 2017. *Unstable Majorities: Polarization, Party Sorting, and Political Stalemate.* Stanford, CA: Hoover Institution Press.

Fiorina, Morris P., and Samuel J. Abrams. 2008. "Political polarization in the American public." *Annual Review of Political Science* 11: 563–588.

Fish, M. Steven. 2005. *Democracy Derailed in Russia: The Failure of Open Politics*. New York: Cambridge University Press.

Florida, Richard. 2016. "How America's metro areas voted." *City Lab*, November 29. www.citylab.com/equity/2016/11/how-americas-metro-areas-voted/508355/ (accessed October 3, 2020).

Foa, Roberto Stefan. 2018. "Modernization and authoritarianism." *Journal of Democracy* 29(3): 129–140.

Fomina, Joanna, and Jacek Kucharczyk. 2016. "Populism and protest in Poland." *Journal of Democracy* 27(4): 56–68.

Freedom House. 2005. *Freedom in the World 2005: Russia*. https://freedom house.org/report/freedom-world/2005/russia (accessed January 8, 2020).

2016. *Freedom in the World: Hungary*. https://freedomhouse.org/report/free dom-world/2016/hungary (accessed January 8, 2020).

2020. *Freedom in the World 2020*. https://freedomhouse.org/report/freedom-world (accessed January 8, 2020).

Frum, David. 2017. "How to build an autocracy." *The Atlantic*, March, pp. 48–59.

Fukuyama, Francis. 1989. "The end of history?" *National Interest* 16: 3–18.

Geddes, Barbara, Joseph Wright, and Erica Frantz. 2018. *How Dictatorships Work*. New York: Cambridge Univeristy Press.

Gibson, Edward L. 2012. *Boundary Control: Subnational Authoritarianism in Federal Democracies*. New York: Cambridge University Press.

Ginsburg, Tom, and Alberto Simpser, eds. 2014. *Constitutions in Authoritarian Regimes*. New York: Cambridge University Press.

Ginsburg, Tom and Aziz Z. Huq. 2018. *How to Save a Constitutional Democracy*. Chicago, IL: University of Chicago Press.

Golder, Matt. 2016. "Far Right Parties in Europe." *Annual Review of Political Science* 19: 477–497.

Graber, Mark A., Sanford Levinson, and Mark Tushnet, eds., 2018. *Constitutional Democracy in Crisis?* New York: Oxford University Press.

Graham, Matthew, and Milan Svolik. 2019. "Democracy in America? Partisanship, polarization and the robustness of support for democracy in the United States." Social Science Research Network. https://papers.ssrn.com/sol3/papers.cfm?abstract_id=3354559 (accessed April 10, 2020).

Grzymala-Busse, Anna. 2019. "How populists rule: The consequence for democratic governance." *Polity* 51(4): 707–717.

Guriev, Sergei, and Daniel Treisman. 2019. "Informational autocrats." *Journal of Economic Perspectives* 33(4): 100–127.

Haggard, Stephan and Robert R. Kaufman. 1995. *The Political Economy of Democratic Transitions*. Princeton, NJ. Princeton University Press.

2012. "Inequality and regime change: Democratic transitions and the stability of democratic rule." *American Political Science Review* 106(3): 495–516.

2016. *Dictators and Democrats: Masses, Elites, and Regime Change*. Princeton, NJ: Princeton University Press.

Hajnal, Zoltan L., Elisabeth R. Gerber, and Hugh Louch. 2002. "Minorities and direct legislation: Evidence from California ballot proposition elections." *Journal of Politics* 64(1): 154–177.

Hennessey, Susan and Benjamin Wittes. 2020. *Unmaking the Presidency: Donald Trump's War on the World's Most Powerful Office*. New York: Farrar, Straus and Giroux.

Hunter, Wendy, and Timothy J. Power. 2019. "Bolsonaro and Brazil's illiberal backlash." *Journal of Democracy* 30(1): 68–82.

Huntington, Samuel P. 1993. *The Third Wave: Democratization in the Late Twentieth Century*. Norman: University of Oklahoma Press.

Iyengar, Shanto, and Sean J. Westwood. 2015. "Fear and loathing across party lines: New evidence on group polarization." *American Journal of Political Science* 59(3): 690–707.

Jamieson, Kathleen Hall. 2018. *Cyberwar: How Russian Trolls Helped Elect a President*. New York: Oxford University Press.

Jasiewicz, Krzysztof. 2008. "The new populism in Poland: The usual suspects?" *Problems of Post-communism* 55(3): 7–25.

Kaufman, Robert R., and Stephan Haggard. 2019. "Democratic decline in the United States: What can we learn from middle-income backsliding?" *Perspectives on Politics* 17(2): 417–432.

Kelemen, R. Daniel. 2017. "Europe's other democratic deficit: National authoritarianism in Europe's democratic union." *Government and Opposition* 52(2): 1–28.

2019. "Is differentiation possible in rule of law?" *Comparative European Politics* 17(2): 246–260.

Kenny, Paul. 2017. *Populism and Patronage: Why Populists Win Elections in India, Asia and Beyond*. New York: Oxford University Press.

2019. *Populism in Southeast Asia*. New York: Cambridge University Press.

Keyman, E. Fuat, and Sebnem Gumuscu. 2014. *Democracy, Identity, and Foreign Policy in Turkey: Hegemony through Transformation*. London: Palgrave Macmillan.

Kingsley, Patrick. 2018. "As West fears the rise of autocrats, Hungary shows what's possible." *New York Times*, February 10. www.nytimes.com/2018/02/10/world/europe/hungary-orban-democracy-far-right.html?smprod=nytcore-ipad&smid=nytcore-ipad-share.

Knuckey, Jonathan, and Myunghee Kim. "Evaluations of Michelle Obama as First Lady: The role of racial resentment." *Presidential Studies Quarterly* 46(2): 365–386.

Lessig, Lawrence. 2018. *America, Compromised*. Chicago, IL: University of Chicago Press.

Levitsky, Steven, and Lucan A. Way. 2010. *Competitive Authoritarianism: Hybrid Regimes after the Cold War*. New York: Cambridge University Press.

2015. "The myth of democratic recession." *Journal of Democracy* 26(1): 45–58.

Levitsky, Steven, and Daniel Ziblatt. 2018. *How Democracies Die*. New York: Broadway Books.

Lindblom, Charles. 1977. *Politics and Markets*. New York: Basic Books.

Linz, Juan José, Alfred Stepan, and Arturo Valenzuela, eds. 1978. *The Breakdown of Democratic Regimes*, vol. 1. Baltimore, MD: Johns Hopkins University Press.

Lindberg, Staffan. 2018. "The nature of backsliding in Europe." Carnegie Europe, July 24. https://carnegieeurope.eu/2018/07/24/nature-of-democratic-backsliding-in-europe-pub–76868 (accessed January 8, 2020).

Lueders, Hans, and Ellen Lust. 2018. "Multiple measurements, elusive agreement, and unstable outcomes in the study of regime change." *Journal of Politics* 80(2): 736–741.

Lührmann, Anna, Marcus Tannenberg, and Staffan I. Lindberg. 2018. "Regimes of the World (RoW): Opening new avenues for the comparative study of political regimes." *Politics and Governance* 6.1: 60–77.

Mann, Thomas E., and Norman J. Ornstein. 2012. *It's Even Worse than It Looks: How the American Constitutional System Collided with the New Politics of Extremism*. New York: Basic Books,

Magyar, Bálint. 2016. *Post-communist Mafia State*. Budapest: Central European University Press.

Mainwaring, Scott and Aníbal Pérez-Liñán. 2014. *Democracies and Dictatorships in Latin America: Emergence, Survival, and Fall* New York: Cambridge University Press.

Mainwaring, Scott, and Fernando Bizzarro. 2019. "The fates of third-wave democracies." *Journal of Democracy* 30(1): 99–113.

Mann, Thomas E., and Norman J. Ornstein. 2012. "Let's just say it: The Republicans are the problem." *Washington Post*, April 27.

Markowski, Radoslaw. 2016. "The Polish parliamentary election of 2015: A free and fair election that results in unfair political consequences." *West European Politics* 39(6): 1311–1322.

Marshall, Monty G., Ted Robert Gurr, and Keith Jaggers. 2019. *Polity IV Project Political Regime Characteristics and Transitions, 1800–2018.* www.systemicpeace.org/inscrdata.html (accessed October 3, 2020).

Mayer, Jane. 2017. *Dark Money: The Hidden History of the Billionaires behind the Rise of the Radical Right.* New York: Anchor Books.

McCarty, Nolan. 2019. *Polarization: What Everyone Needs to Know.* New York: Oxford University Press.

McCarty, Nolan, Keith T. Poole, and Howard Rosenthal. 2016. *Polarized America: The Dance of Ideology and Unequal Riches.* Cambridge, MA: MIT Press.

McCoy, Jennifer, Tahmina Rahman, and Murat Somer. 2018. "Polarization and the global crisis of democracy: Common patterns, dynamics, and pernicious consequences for democratic polities." *American Behavioral Scientist* 62(1): 16–42.

McFaul, Michael. 2001. *Russia's Unfinished Revolution: Political Change from Gorbachev to Putin.* Ithaca, NY: Cornell University Press.

Mechkova, Valeriya, Anna Lührmann, and Staffan I. Lindberg. 2017. "How much democratic backsliding?" *Journal of Democracy* 28(4): 162–169.

Meunier, Sophie, and Milada Anna Vachudova. 2018. "Liberal intergovernmentalism, illiberalism and the potential superpower of the European Union." *Journal of Common Market Studies* 56(7): 1631–1647.

Mickey, Robert, Steven Levitsky, and Lucan Ahmad Way. 2017. "Is America still safe for democracy: Why the United States is in danger of backsliding." *Foreign Affairs* 96: 20.

Morgan, Stephen L., and Jiwon Lee. 2017. "The white working class and voter turnout in US presidential elections, 2004 to 2016." *Sociological Science* 4: 656–685.

Mounk, Yascha. 2018. *The People vs. Democracy: Why Our Freedom Is in Danger and How to Save It.* Cambridge, MA: Harvard University Press.

Mudde, Cas, and Cristóbal Rovira Kaltwasser. 2017. *Populism: A Very Short Introduction.* Oxford: Oxford University Press.

Neiwert, David. 2017. *Alt-America: The Rise of the Radical Right in the Age of Trump.* London: Verso Books.

Norris, Pippa. 2014. *Why Electoral Integrity Matters.* Cambridge: Cambridge University Press.

Norris, Pipa, and Ronald Inglehart. 2018. *Cultural Backlash and the Rise of Populist Authoritarianism.* Cambridge: Cambridge University Press.

O'Connor, Cailin and James Owen Weatherall. 2019. *The Misinformation Age: How False Beliefs Spread*. New Haven, CT: Yale Univeristy Press.

O'Donnell, Guillermo. 2004. "The quality of democracy: Why the rule of law matters." *Journal of Democracy* 15(4): 32–46.

Orenstein, Mitchell A., Péter Krekó and Attila Juhász. 2015. "The Hungarian Putin? Viktor Orbán and the Kremlin's playbook." *Foreign Affairs*, February 8.

Ottaway, Marina. 2003. *Democracy Challenged; The Rise of Semi-Authoritarianism*. Washington, DC. Carnegie Endowment for International Peace.

Pew Research Center. 2019. "Partisan antipathy: More intense, more personal: Majority of Republicans say Democrats are 'more unpatriotic' than other Americans." October 10. www.people-press.org/2019/10/10/partisan-antipathy-more-intense-more-personal, (accessed October 3, 2020).

Powell, Jonathan M., and Clayton L. Thyne. 2011. "Global instances of coups from 1950 to 2010: A new dataset." *Journal of Peace Research* 48(2): 249–259.

Pomerantsev, Peter. 2019. *This is Not Propaganda: Adventures in the War Against Reality*. New York: Public Affairs.

Przeworski, Adam. 2019. *Crises of Democracy*. New York: Cambridge University Press.

Przeworski, Adam, Susan C. Stokes, and Bernard Manin, eds. 1999. *Democracy, Accountability, and Representation*. Cambridge: Cambridge University Press.

Przeworski, Adam, et al. 2000. *Democracy and Development: Political Institutions and Well-Being in the World, 1950–1990*. New York: Cambridge University Press.

Remington, Thomas F. 2008. *The Russian Parliament: Institutional Evolution in a Transitional Regime, 1989–1999*. New Haven, CT: Yale University Press.

Rhodes-Purdy, Matthew, and Raul L. Madrid. 2020. "The perils of personalism." *Democratization* 27(2): 321–339.

Rothwell, Jonathan T., and Pablo Diego-Rosell. 2017. "Explaining Nationalist Political Views: The Case of Donald Trump." SSRN: https://ssrn.com/abstract=2822059 or http://dx.doi.org/10.2139/ssrn.2822059 (accessed October 3, 2020).

Sartori, Giovanni. 1966. "European Political Parties: The Case of Polarized Pluralism." In *Political Parties and Political Development*, edited by Jason LaPalombara and Myron Weiner, pp. 136–176. Princeton, NJ: Princeton University Press.

Schedler, Andreas. 2002. "Elections Without Democracy: The Menu of Manipulation." *Journal of Democracy* 13 (2): 36–50.

2009. "Electoral authoritarianism." In *The SAGE Handbook of Comparative Politics*, edited by Todd Landman and Neil Robinson, pp. 381–394. Newbury Park, CA: Sage Publishers.

Schedler, Andreas, Larry Diamond, and Marc F. Plattner, eds. 1999. *The Self-Restraining State: Power and Accountability in New Democracies*. Boulder, CO. Lynne Reiner Publishers.

Scheppele, Kim Lane. 2013. "The rule of law and the Frankenstate: Why governance checklists do not work." *Governance* 26(4): 559–562.

Schumpeter, Joseph. 1962. *Capitalism, Socialism and Democracy*. New York: Harper Perennial.

Schickler, Eric. 2016. *Racial Realignment: The Transformation of American Liberalism, 1932–1965*. Princeton, NJ: Princeton University Press.

Shleifer, Andrei, and Daniel Treisman. 2005. "A normal country: Russia after communism." *Journal of Economic Perspectives* 19(1): 151–174.

Skocpol, Theda, and Vanessa Williamson. 2016. *The Tea Party and the Remaking of Republican Conservatism*. New York: Oxford University Press.

Snyder, Richard. 2019. *Inside Countries: Subnational Research in Comparative Politics*. Cambridge: Cambridge University Press.

Stanley, Jason (2015). *How Propaganda Works*. Princeton, NJ: Princeton University Press.

Stoyan, Alissandra T. 2015. "Ambitious reform via constituent assemblies: Determinants of success in contemporary Latin America." *Studies in Comparative International Development* 55: 99–121.

Sunstein, Cass R., ed. 2018a. *Can It Happen Here? Authoritarianism in America*. New York: Harper and Collins

Sunstein, Cass R. 2018b. *#Republic: Divided Democracy in the Age of Social Media*. Princeton, NJ: Princeton University Press.

Svolik, Milan. 2008. "Authoritarian reversals and democratic consolidation." *American Political Science Review* 102(2): 153–168.

2009. "Power sharing and leadership dynamics in authoritarian regimes." *American Journal of Political Science* 53(2): 477–494.

2018. "When polarization trumps civic virtue: Partisan conflict and the subversion of democracy by incumbents." SSRN: https://papers.ssrn.com /sol3/papers.cfm?abstract_id=3243470 (accessed October 3, 2020).

Szczerbiak, Aleks. 2017. "Power without love: Patterns of party politics in post-1989 Poland." In *Post-Communist EU Member States*, edited by Susanne Jungerstom-Mulders, pp. 105–138. New York: Routledge.

Tansey, Oisin. 2016. *The International Politics of Authoritarian Rule*. New York: Oxford University Press.

Tesler, Michael. 2016. *Post-racial or Most-Racial? Race and Politics in the Obama Era*. Chicago, IL: University of Chicago Press.

Treisman, Daniel, and Andrei Shleifer. 2004. "A normal country." *Foreign Affairs* 83(2): 20–38.

Tushnet, Mark. 2015. "Authoritarian Constitutionalism." *Cornell Law Review* 100: 391–461.

Urbinati, Nadia. 2019. *Me the People: How Populism Transforms Democracy*. Cambridge, MA: Harvard University Press.

Vachudova, Milada Ann. 2020. "Ethnopopulism and democratic backsliding in Central Europe." *East European Politics* 36(3): 318–340.

Waldner, David, and Ellen Lust. 2018. "Unwelcome change: Coming to terms with democratic backsliding." *Annual Review of Political Science* 21: 93–113.

Winters, Jeffrey A. 2011. *Oligarchy*. New York: Cambridge University Press.

Yabanci, Bilge. 2016. "Populism as the problem child of democracy: The AKP's enduring appeal and the use of meso-level actors." *Southeast Europe and Black Sea Studies* 16(4): 591–617.

Weyland, Kurt. 2001 "Clarifying a contested concept: Populism in the study of Latin American politics." *Comparative Politics* 34(1): 1–22.

Zakaria, Fareed. 1997. "The rise of illiberal democracy." *Foreign Affairs* 76: 22.

Zakaria, Fareed. 2007. *The Future of Freedom: Illiberal Democracy at Home and Abroad*. New York: WW Norton & company.

Ziblatt, Daniel. 2017. *Conservative Political Parties and the Birth of Modern Democracy in Europe*. Cambridge: Cambridge University Press.

Acknowledgments

We would like to thank Mikhail Alexseev, Senem Aydın-Düzgit, Michael Bernard, Mariana Carvalho, Catherine Conaghan, Javier Corrales, Jasmina Dimitrieva, Jesse Driscoll, Zsolt Enyedi, Berk Esen, Leo Falabella, Richard Feinberg, Clark Gibson, Tom Ginsburg, Gary Goertz, Eric Gordy, Peter Gourevitch, Béla Greskovitz, Anna Grzymala-Busse, Sebnem Gumuscu, Henry Hale, Peter Hall, Jonathan Hartlyn, Robert Hayden, Gary Jacobson, Krzysztof Jasiewicz, Stathis Kalyvas, Daniel Keleman, Adrienne Lebas, Raul Madrid, Scott Mainwaring, Matthias Matthijs, Sebastian Mazzuca, Jennifer McCoy, Harris Mylonas, Ziya Öniş, Takis Pappas, Rachel Beatty Riedl, Philip Roeder, Wojciech Sadurski, Andrew Schranck, Brigitte Seim, Matthew Shugart, Jack Snyder, Murat Somer, Dimitrios Sotiropoulos, David Stasavage, Dersu Tanca, Lydia Tiede, Daniel Treisman, Hubert Tworzecki, Milada Vuchodova, Michael Wahman, Lucan Way, Sotiris Zartaloudis and participants in several seminars at the London School of Economics. Our thanks to Inbok Rhee and Terence Teo for their committed research assistance as well as the contributions of Giovanni Angioni and Liuya Zhang and outstanding copy-editing from Kit Haggard.

Cambridge Elements ☰

Political Economy

David Stasavage
New York University

David Stasavage is Julius Silver Professor in the Wilf Family Department of Politics at New York University. He previously held positions at the London School of Economics and at Oxford University. His work has spanned a number of different fields and currently focuses on two areas: development of state institutions over the long run and the politics of inequality. He is a member of the American Academy of Arts and Sciences.

About the Series

The Element Series Political Economy provides authoritative contributions on important topics in the rapidly growing field of political economy. Elements are designed so as to provide broad and in depth coverage combined with original insights from scholars in political science, economics, and economic history. Contributions are welcome on any topic within this field.

Cambridge Elements $\equiv$

Political Economy

Elements in the Series

State Capacity and Economic Development: Present and Past
Mark Dincecco

Nativism and Economic Integration Across the Developing World: Collision and Accommodation
Rikhil R. Bhavnani and Bethany Lacina

Lynching and Local Justice: Legitimacy and Accountability in Weak States
Danielle F. Jung and Dara Kay Cohen

The Economic Origin of Political Parties
Christopher Kam and Adlai Newson

A full series listing is available at: www.cambridge.org/EPEC

Printed in the United States
By Bookmasters